A Thousand Feasts

Also by Nigel Slater:

A Cook's Book
Greenfeast
The Christmas Chronicles
The Kitchen Diaries III
Eat
The Kitchen Diaries II
Tender, Volumes I and II
Eating for England
The Kitchen Diaries
Toast: The story of a boy's hunger
Appetite
Real Food
Real Cooking
The 30-Minute Cook
Real Fast Puddings
Real Fast Food

A Thousand Feasts

Small moments of joy
… a memoir of sorts

Nigel Slater

4th ESTATE · *London*

4th Estate
An imprint of HarperCollins*Publishers*
1 London Bridge Street
London SE1 9GF

www.4thestate.co.uk

HarperCollins*Publishers*
Macken House, 39/40 Mayor Street Upper
Dublin 1, D01 C9W8, Ireland

First published in Great Britain in 2024 by 4th Estate

24 25 26 27 28 LBC 6 5 4 3 2

For James

Contents

Acknowledgements   ix

Notes, stories and small moments of joy   1

With spoon in hand   5

Packing a suitcase   97

Making home   153

The hands of a cook   211

Through the garden gate   255

A little more   325

Acknowledgements

I am not sure how you even start to acknowledge those responsible for a lifetime of joyous memories, so I can only bow, long and deep, to everyone who has brought about the events I mention on the pages that follow. It would have been a much-diminished life without you.

Printed words of gratitude rarely seem enough but once again I thank my editor Louise Haines for her patience, encouragement and wise words. To Michelle Kane for her continuing, boundless support and enthusiasm and to everyone at 4th Estate, my publishers for thirty years, especially Julian Humphries and Alex Gingell, Vic Pullen, Linden Lawson and Holly Kyte. Once again, my thanks to David Pearson.

My life has revolved around my weekly *Observer* column for three decades, and I thank the wonderful Allan Jenkins and everyone at *The Observer* for their continuing support. I am, as always, grateful to my literary agents Araminta Whitley and Ben Clark and everyone at The Soho Agency.

Thank you to the potters whose pieces I use in my home every day and make cooking and eating such a pleasure, especially Florian Gadsby, Steve Harrison and Anne Mette Hjortshøj. And to Jennifer Lee and Edmund de Waal without whose works my home would just not be the same.

Many of the feasts between these covers have occurred during my times in Japan. To all those who welcome me there each year I offer my gratitude, especially Takahiro Yagi, Kyoko Kuga and

Takako Saito. My gratitude to Tim d'Offay and everyone at Postcard Teas in London and to Lyn Harris and her team at Perfumer H for their friendship and enjoyable collaborations. A big shout out to George Ashwell and everyone at The Lighthouse Club for their support and encouragement.

This book is, as always, for James Thompson. Its purpose has, from the start, been to share good times with others. Many of the moments recorded here have been shared with James, especially those in Iran and in Lebanon where he continues his work with The Great Oven, his network for helping those living in areas of conflict. James, how could I even begin to thank you?

And to all those who follow me on Instagram and Bluesky social platforms, thank you, thank you, lovely people. Your support is deeply appreciated.

Notes, stories and small moments of joy

There is so much to feast on. The sight of a wave of snowdrops under the gnarled branches of an oak tree; the crisp pages of a new diary; a battered wicker basket of dumplings fresh from the steamer. I feast on the pleasure of packing for a trip away from home; tucking into an impromptu picnic of bread and cheese; the scent of a bunch of home-grown sweet peas and the satisfaction of a neat pile of fresh ironing. Tiny feasts, but as enriching to me as a laden table with a gathering of boisterous and much-loved friends. These diminutive pleasures are there if we care to look for them, little joys illuminating an increasingly darkening world. They feed the soul and nourish the spirit. Or at least they do mine.

As well as kitchen diaries – the written record of what I cook and eat – I keep notebooks. Details of a life lived mostly in the kitchen, but which also tell of time spent in the garden, on trains and planes, of life at home and away. Between their timeworn covers are recipes and shopping lists, receipts and plans, illegible words and, very occasionally, passages of flowing calligraphy. Many moments are preserved only in a single sentence.

Each note is a memory, written down so I wouldn't forget it. These are not detailed accounts of major events but recordings of something altogether more ephemeral. The sort of moments likely to become misty with time, a jumble of curiosities and wonderings penned at my kitchen table, whilst soaked to the skin in a fisherman's hut in Reykjavík, sitting calmly in a moss garden in Japan or sheltering from a blizzard in the warmth of a chocolate-box Konditorei in Vienna.

This is no neat row of meticulously scripted, leatherbound note-books. What I have is an untidy bundle of haphazard observations, notes and stories kept in pocketbooks and cheap ring-bound note-pads, scribbled on envelopes and loose scraps of paper. There is a faded pink exercise book bought in Delhi whose pencilled essays are now but ghosts. Several manilla-covered schoolbooks and a blue ring-bound journal whose pages are foxed and curled from years spent in the warmth of the kitchen. Many are held together with sticky tape and string. Some written in pencil have faded, those fragments gone for ever; others are etched so brightly in my memory as to be unforgettable.

The thread that binds them is their spirit, a need to keep a writ-ten record of the good things, memories of meals shared or eaten alone, of journeys and places, events and happenings, small things that have given pleasure before they disappeared. Each one is, I suppose, a short story to remind me of something, ordinary or extraordinary, that I felt worth chronicling. They are, almost with-out exception, moments of quiet jubilation: a ripe mango eaten in a rainstorm; the smell of incense in a temple or the sound of foot-steps on the stone floor of an abbey. They are chronicles of quietness and calm, busy days in the kitchen and sensuous after-noons spent in the garden.

Readers hoping for tales of riotous tables and gluttonous orgies (and who clearly don't know this author very well) may be disap-pointed. I have always been happier writing about treacle falling off a spoon than tracking and killing my own dinner. And whilst other writers concern themselves with the broader picture – and thank goodness they do – I have spent my cooking life recording only the smallest of observations, because it is those tiny, intimate details of life that fascinate me.

It must be said that I record only the best bits of this life.

Moments of gold that can last an entire evening or be over in a flash. I see no point in putting pen to paper to preserve anything negative, sad or painful. Heaven knows, there is enough of that. I have no wish to live in a rose-tinted bubble, but if I have learned one thing, it is not only to concentrate on the the 'positive stuff', but to cherish it. I will admit to seeking it out, to looking up instead of down, to being curious and to hold on, as tightly as I can, to 'the good things', however small. This is why I have put these stories, paragraphs and lines – these brief celebrations, each one a tiny feast – together as a collection.

What you have in your hands is a ragbag collection of some of the happiest of times, the small moments of joy that have been the seasoning in this cook's stew. A little box of curiosities to dip into, to comfort and to distract, albeit briefly, from more complicated times. They are collected not only for myself (though I admit there is something of that here), but so that others may, I hope, derive joy from them too.

With spoon in hand

Mangoes in a monsoon
Varca Beach, Goa

I drift in and out of sleep in the back seat. Slow, deep breaths, in and out like the tide. I am woken by the crack of a twig hitting the windscreen and the driver snaps at me to close my window. In a heartbeat, the roof of the car is being pounded by raindrops the size of cherries, the windscreen wipers splashing hysterically. Swishshtock, swish-shtock. The ancient coconut palms, once so wise and calm, are now swaying back and forth, their leaves flapping like elephants' ears.

We stop. The driver can no longer see the road ahead, let alone negotiate its potholes. I am wondering whether the roof of his immaculate, ancient Morris Oxford, with its crocheted antimacassars washed and ironed daily by his mother, can take the force of the rain or if the engine will flood. Rain has always felt like a benign occurrence, even more so here, but this is a whole new level of rain. I feel tiny, threatened.

There is a pile of small, round mangoes on the passenger seat. The driver passes one over his shoulder and I grab it like a life raft. I watch as he rips lumps of turmeric-yellow flesh with his teeth. He eats his mango like an apple, spitting the skin into his left hand. I follow suit.

Just as there is rain and 'rain', there are mangoes and 'mangoes'. A trickle of nectar is running down my chin, stinging my naked, sunburnt thighs. The flesh is sweet and honeyed, soft as ice cream. The rain drums on the roof. The sky is charcoal and crimson. Neither of us knows if the car will start again.

As I ponder the etiquette of what to do with the sucked-clean stone and its orange beard, the car sways back and forth like a rocking horse and we start to laugh hysterically. It crosses my mind that there may be worse ways to die than in a monsoon, laughing, with mango juice on your lips.

A tiny cube of soft tofu the colour of buttermilk. On its surface a small pea of green wasabi and a single pickled cherry blossom. It sits in a clear, glistening moat of ponzu sauce on an old blue-and-white dish. I have genuinely never seen anything more beautiful.

Appams in Galle
Sri Lanka

Thin, like paper, light and doughy in the middle, crisp and delicate as honeycomb at the edges, the appam is tempting even before it is filled with a ladle of lush vegetable curry. It shares many of the attributes of a pikelet or crumpet, a round disc of batter, bland and comforting, but stretched until its edges are as fine and crisp as Belgian lace. Of all the yeasted dough goods throughout the world, the appam is the lightest and, at its best, the most fragile.

The one that landed on my tray in Galle last night was a work of art, the accompanying curry mild and sweetened with coconut, as is the way with much coastal cooking. The terracotta sauce goes some way to tempering my anger at the way the owners have stripped the hotel of its antique furnishings, even its original doors, selling to eager antique dealers from all over the world who turn up at this ancient hotel, bundles of cash in hand.*

I sit on the edge of a cane-backed planter's chair in the lobby, doors open, watery morning sun meandering in, writing my diary. Someone is blasting Montserrat Caballé from one of the hotel bedrooms. I have just been brought a glass of mango juice as thick as treacle. It is hard to think of a more perfect start to a day. Monserrat Caballé *and* a ripe mango. I do not deserve this life.

---

* Years later, it seems as if the antique strippers may have done the world, if not the hotel, a favour, when a horrific tsunami causes serious flooding to the hotel and devastation to many of the surrounding buildings. At least something has been saved, albeit in a luxury apartment in Florida.

The chef who made dinner last night comes over to say hello. We discuss the art of making appam. He offers to show me how, and I follow him like a lamb to the kitchen. As when making a pancake, the lightness depends not only on the right batter recipe, the details of which he is a little hazy about – but the deftness of using an old *appachatti*, the blackened steel pan like a thick, two-handled wok. He pours batter in and then most of it out again, leaving only the thinnest layer attached to the sides. There is much swivelling wrist action, which I try to repeat when I am left to have a go myself. The result – his, a wafer of minute holes, frilled at the edge; mine, a thick, soggy pancake as fine and delicate as a bath sponge, which he assures me is not bad for a first attempt. Amidst the thanks, and a gift of a new *appachatti*, I make a mental note to stick to making crumpets.

A lamb feast
Beqaa Valley, Lebanon

We drag an assortment of tables into the courtyard, pushing them together on the uneven floor. They fit together awkwardly, some taller than others, a wobbly leg here and there. One of the camp's resident artists has painted the longest of the tables with red-and-yellow butterflies on a vivid blue background. Someone scatters plastic plates around, gold-rimmed, adorned with roses in pink and turquoise. We will drink from paper cups and eat with spoons.

Shallow glass bowls the size of steering wheels are brought from the kitchen, piled with steaming rice, yellow turnips and lumps of stewed lamb still on its bones. Round the edge a ring of crisp, brown falafel, each one a perfectly pointed egg of wheat, thyme and minced onions. Bowls of palest yellow sauce – a mixture of the cooking juices from the meat, turmeric and yoghurt – are squeezed between piles of warm flatbreads, like vast pancakes, crumpled like bedsheets. There are plastic bottles of water and orange squash, no alcohol.

Music issues from a dusty ghetto blaster, a hypnotic Lebanese rock that I try unsuccessfully to Shazam on the dodgy internet for later. My plate of sharp yellow sauce, a Fabergé egg of falafel and fried fat cashews has a blue rose peeping out from under the mound of silky long-grain rice. I suck the meat from the thin rib bones and spoon the cooking liquor and yoghurt over my rice.

The conversation is at first hushed, confined to whispers in Arabic, French and English. We are artists, cooks and musicians,

11

locals and some who are far, far from home. Dishes are passed round the table. Water, bowls of sauce, pieces of lamb and warm rice are greeted with soft murmurs of appreciation.

As the sun sets, the conversation rises slowly to a joyful hubbub, a quietly excited babble, until it reaches the point where you can hear only the person at your side. Anywhere else, I would attribute this to the alcohol kicking in. But here it is down to the food and the joy of sharing it.

As the sky turns to lilac and saffron, bats swoop above our heads, crows come to rest on the jagged roofs of ruined buildings whose plaster is cracked and riddled with holes. In the distance there is the sound of explosions, the constant reminder of how close we are to Syria. For now, at least, we feast.

Breakfast on the terrace, Lebanon. A square of white sheep's milk cheese on a white plate, moist, crumbly with the clean, sharp tang of sour milk. I trickle liquid honey over the craggy surface, letting it fall slowly from the spoon and watching as it forms tiny pools of gold in the cheese's creases and dimples.

Piper nigrum
Malabar Coast

I could barely see them at first. Then, a flash of billowing saffron cloth in the deep-green undergrowth. Another, purple this time, then a white headband and a black-and-beige striped shirt like a humbug. The pepper pickers are two metres above my head, balancing on bamboo ladders tied together with raffia, partially hidden by the pepper plants' lush vines.

I am at one of the Malabar Coast's many pepper plantations, yet all I can see is mile after mile of neatly clipped camelia bushes, looking for all the world like well-curated topiary. The bushes turn out to be tea (so I was right about them being camelias; the pepper is growing on vines that climb tall silver oaks dotted throughout the plantation). Pepper is an intercrop, making its home amongst tea bushes high in the mountains. This is a place that has never seen snow, frost or hail, and as we climb higher still the peppercorns hang in long clusters from the tree trunks, each sprig sporting everything from green berries no bigger than a pinhead to ripe red ones and fat black-brown berries. It takes seven months to go from tiny star-like flowers to ripe fruit.

The pickers are, today, collecting only the aubergine and brown berries, all of which are destined become dried peppercorns in my mill by the stove. (Green berries may be picked fresh, to be pickled in brine.) There are up to three pickers round the trunk of every tree, each carefully pulling off a sprig of ripening peppercorns and passing it behind his back into the pale-yellow sack tied round his waist. With both hands free, he can use one to lift the

13

thick leaves and the other to pluck the little sprays of berries from underneath.

It is teatime, and the workers sit down in a circle, chattering excitedly, no doubt at the funny guy who has come to watch them work. I decline the offer of chai – too dark and milky for me – and am met with a look of utter amazement.

Later, I see the pepper berries being dried outdoors in the baking sun on vast woven mats. I crush some of the freshly dried peppercorns and tip them into my hand. I breathe in. My nose prickles as sharply as if I have stepped outside on a frosty winter morning. The air smells of lemon and menthol and something dark and almost burnt, like smoky lapsang souchong tea. The smell is closer to perfume than spice, perhaps a whiff of good old-fashioned aftershave, and a very long way from the black dust in a pepper pot. Indeed, a long way from my 'freshly ground pepper' grinder too.

These fleeting scents, of nutmeg from the tree (a breath of Elizabethan pink), turmeric roots in sacks at the spice market (a whiff of ginger and second-hand bookshops), or the lemon and pepper hit of pale, plump fresh ginger root are something I have savoured only briefly. It is not every day one finds oneself in the cardamom hills. You really do need to close your eyes and bathe your senses in those essential oils. You will never forget them – at least I haven't – no matter how briefly you are immersed in them. Perhaps the most elusive tiny feast of all, but one that will remain printed on the memory, like a tattoo.

Slowly tearing apart a cinnamon bun in a coffee shop.

Coffee in Nakazakicho
Osaka, Japan

There are 'hell-on-earth' shopping malls and wide pedestrian walkways that weave high above the city's traffic. There are dark, steaming alleyways where every doorway leads you to a memorable dinner, museums where visitors must be silent and bars so noisy that bar staff have learned to lip-read. To be here on a rainy night is like being on the set of *Blade Runner*.

There is little left of old Osaka. I am pottering around Nakazakicho, what remains of the traditional, narrow streets of the city. Each doorway surrounded by a cute cluster of pots, trailing scented geraniums, shuttlecock ferns and lemon trees. There is a curiously spooky tableau of the area, like a brick nativity, set near the Meditation Centre, which I use to get my bearings. (Google Maps is frustratingly patchy in Japan.) Crates of empty bottles lie neatly stacked outside the shuttered bars, evidence of the area's nightlife. All is closed now except for the public bathhouse and a couple of convenience stores.

Signs of life are few at nine in the morning, but there are low lights and shadowy figures moving in the coffee shops and the smell of roasting coffee beans in the crisp autumn air. The most traditional of them has china cats in the window, hand-made models of pink and pistachio cupcakes under glass domes and a dark, intriguing interior, but it seems reluctant to open. A newer shop, all pale Scandinavian wood, is clearly roasting on the premises and I join the short, enthusiastic queue photographing one another for social media.

The good coffee comes in a tiny china cup instead of the usual hideous mugs, but I am intrigued by the almost unanimous order that is brought to every table – a crème caramel topped with a ball of ice cream whose precarious assembly is reminiscent of Pierrot's pointed hat. Curious, I order one and find it is not the horror I had expected but a delicious collision of two classic desserts, affogato al caffè and crème caramel. Both are of fine quality, as is the hot coffee poured over the top, softening the vanilla ice cream and merging into gorgeous cream and brown swooshes on the plate. I am hooked.

In Hokkaido, a tangle of wild mountain greens in tempura batter, presented on a disc of white paper, like a flower preserved in ice.

Queuing for flatbreads
Tehran

Even at dawn it hurts to breathe. A fiery red ribbon pierces the throat-stinging smog.

We walk to the bakery following the trees for shade, then stand in a loose queue of surly men, the morning air cool around our bare ankles. Somewhere, not too far off, is the sound of running water.

We step into the shop and the temperature rises. The whiteness dazzles. There are clean tiles, sacks of flour and young bearded bakers in white shirts and floor-length aprons. In the rear wall, two jagged slits, large enough to take the wooden-handled paddles, each with their long, thin cargo of dough. Through each opening sheets of bread bake on glowing pebbles.

The dough has been proving overnight, putty-coloured domes with bubbles the size of goose eggs. The baker twists off lumps of dough and teases them into long, foot-wide ribbons. He slides them into the oven with a long-handled peel where they sit, briefly, on the scorching pebbles.

The sheets of sangak – the name means 'little stones' in Farsi – are notched and dented from their time on the knubbly floor of the oven and are moved from oven to counter with an oven glove. Each is tapped firmly to remove any embedded shrapnel, then folded neatly, swiftly in two, then four. Each customer leaves with their bundle of bread folded and tucked under their arm, like a business-man with his morning newspaper.

You would need an imam's self-control not to tear off a piece of your flatbread and wolf it as you walk. I am filming and so must, to the fury of the queue, go through the whole procedure again. This time I turn the bread away from the camera. I wouldn't want the director to spot the missing corner.

Strings of kettles, gold-coloured or plain aluminium, hang down from an awning in the market. The kettles are linked handle on spout, handle on spout, as if holding hands.

Green shoots
Finland

There is a pot of coarse oat porridge with bilberries, a whole side of smoked salmon on a waney-edged plank and venison black pudding as crumbly as chocolate cake. Nettles are pressed into crispbread like leaves on a frozen pond. A sleigh ride from Lapland, snow falling and faced with the breakfast of my dreams, I spoon cakes of potato and kale onto my plate to eat with slices of beetroot-cured salmon. I drink glowing red lingonberry juice from a shot glass that feels like a transfusion and stir a compote of berries into my yoghurt. I then head out for a walk to the quay and its oxide-red wooden houses.

The autumn light in Oulu is gold, filtered through the trees, birch mostly, their thin white bark peeling from their trunks in sheets, their leaves fluttering with the faintest breeze. The grass beneath, a Persian carpet of green, brown and ochre from the fallen leaves, is moist and peppered with tiny mushrooms. I find myself examining their stems as I did so keenly in my twenties, but these are straight.

Lunch is early and long. Pea soup, grilled Arctic char and a granita of lemon verbena, but as the afternoon light drops, so does the temperature. I have a good scarf and gloves with me but my thermals aren't up to the weather and I head to the roaring fire and a cocktail, the first of which involves lingonberries, spruce shoots and elderflower. A second, there is always a second, gin, spruce and lemon.

The next day, more spruce shoots, this time as shots before breakfast. The needles are the young, soft, lime-green tips from the end of the branches; tufts pliable enough to be whizzed into juice and drunk like wheatgrass. Except that this green liquor isn't bitter, it has a dazzling citrus sourness that I will crave every winter morning from now on.

A wooden rack outside a baker's shop in Stockholm. Floury, rough-edged sheets of knåckebröd, stacked like newspapers, tied with thin blue ribbon.

On being handed a menu

I have arrived almost on time, been settled gently at my table and offered a drink. I may even have it in my hand and have taken that first blissful sip. I have sussed out the room and the prevailing atmosphere; the temperament of the front of house and the good smells coming from the kitchen. I realise – gratefully – that all is going to be well. And then, as if that isn't enough, someone brings a printed list of delights.

A menu is a collection of temptations. A card from which to choose something that someone else will cook. For once, a meal for which I haven't shopped, chopped and done the washing up. Believe me when I say there are few bigger treats for someone who spends so much of their life at the cooker or sink.

Menus are less formal now, shorn of the tyranny of three courses. You can choose two small plates, one larger one or, I would imagine, three puddings, though I cannot pretend I have ever tried. (I may have *thought* about it.) Better still, you can choose, without upsetting the kitchen, a collection of dishes for the table to pick from as the fancy takes you. Sharing food appeals to me. This is how I like to eat in a restaurant – except pudding, of course, which is mine and mine alone. (I say this only to hijack the plans of 'those who don't order dessert', then go on to eat most of mine.)

The first menu from which I was allowed to choose listed fruit juice – pineapple, grapefruit or orange – as a starter. The drinks came in small wine goblets on a plate with a doily. You sipped slowly whilst the grown-ups slurped their soup. Basic, yes, but the excitement of choosing my dinner from a menu, typed and imprisoned in blue leatherette, was unimaginable and what started a lifelong love of restaurants.

Honey, and a bear in the forest
Amir Kola, Iran

You can just see the hives through the swirling smoke, fifty or more of them in a clearing in the forest, each one with faded wooden sides and a stained zinc lid. A few are painted sailboat blue. The smoke is thin and ghostly, the sound of the bees almost drowned out by the rushing water of the tumbling river below us. It is eerie but only in a way that makes you feel you may see a faun, Mr Tumnus perhaps, galloping through the trees.

We have driven for hours into the foothills, looking out for the beehives. Not a soul has crossed our path, and we are ready to give up, feeling we may have missed our way. But the smoke (used to calm the bees) proves a useful guide for the team. Our beekeeper turns out to be a bear of a man with possibly the largest hands I have ever seen. Gentle and benign, as you might expect of someone whose life is marinated in old trees and sweet honey. A man who cares for his bees like they were his children.

Three times now I have worn a beekeeper's suit, the white dungarees, helmet and veil. It feels like walking on the moon. There is no such luxury here, and I stand well clear as the keeper lifts the lid and pulls out one of the wooden 'supers' thick with honeycomb.

We breakfast in the beekeeper's tent with its unmade bed in one corner, a tiny stove and old tin kettle in the other. The honey appears on an oval tin tray, craggy blocks of honeycomb oozing their sticky cargo onto the tray. We scoop the honey up with forks (I looked in vain for a spoon), trying hard not to drip on the tired pink carpet that covers the floor of the tent. The honey is not as sweet as that at home, more liquid, and its fragrance is both floral and resinous.

Perched in the tent on a mountain, surrounded by tall pines, the scent of woodsmoke and the sound of the distant water rushing over rocks like the laughter of happy children, this could well be the breakfast of dreams.

Eating gold
Kanazawa, Japan

The stream, wide and vibrant, winds its way through the gardens, the heavy stones along its way luminous green with moss. Every now and again the stream suddenly crashes down three metres in a small and noisy waterfall.

I have come to visit Kanazawa's Museum of Contemporary Art but I have picked the one day of the week when it is closed. Something all too easy to do in a country whose opening hours are more than a little eccentric. I stop to buy chopsticks as a gift for a friend, and many cups of roasted tea later I walk up the hill to see the cherry blossoms.

They are lovely in the way that all cherry blossom is lovely – pink and frilly and slightly cloying to the eye – but a few steps away from the crowds is a hut selling ice cream. I queue for a cornet, which comes with a perfect soft-serve swirl that is then showered with gold leaf. Tiny snowflakes of gold on a wave of vanilla ice cream that I eat under the cherry trees. Silly, decadent and breathtakingly beautiful.

A gnarled, grey tree whose branches are covered in creamy-white bubbles of opening blossom. It is like a tree festooned with popcorn.

The breakfast buffet
Seoul, South Korea

A seaweed salad like wet pipe tobacco; 'doll's house' maki rolls that I think of as sushi for children; a sticky salad of nattō and a slippery one of raw salmon. There is kimchi of white radish and another of cucumber, a rust-red version with Chinese cabbage and yet another that is a tangle of small white roots, the translation of which leaves me none the wiser.

Purées of plum or dusky berries float on glass pots of yoghurt; scallops and oysters quiver on the half-shell and platters of sashimi sit on jagged crystals of crushed ice. Slices of boiled bacon with a mustard glaze are arranged in a soldierly line; poached white fish is wantonly sprinkled with spring onions; a mixture of aubergines and minced pork and another of hot and leafy mustard greens bask in chafing dishes next to stainless-steel cauldrons of miso soup. There are wicker baskets of dumplings steaming and a whole table of ingredients – rice, eggs, greens and soy sauce – with which to build your own bibimbap.

This is what greets me at breakfast in my hotel in Seoul, along with a trainee chef carefully tending omelettes and another turning out pans of gyoza and another hand-throwing noodles like it was an Olympic sport. This is all before I spot the smoothie stand, a trio of sushi chefs and the pastry section with its miniature croissants and perfectly piped Paris-Brest.

The young American businessman on the next table comes back from the buffet with a bowl of multicoloured Cheerios.

I don't take sugar but keep a special pot for guests. A pale, Korean celadon pot with a hexagonal lid, a gift from a friend. It holds a small enough amount, a mere six or so teaspoons, that make the contents seem precious, as of course sugar once was. It makes me think of the sugar-tasting scene in Jessie Burton's haunting novel *The Miniaturist*, where everyone closed their eyes as they licked the sugar from their teaspoons.

Getting into a pickle

Amongst the kimchi and sauerkraut, yoghurt and kefir on the top shelf of the fridge is a row of glass jars whose contents are the colour of costume jewellery. This is my stash of tsukemono, the Japanese pickled vegetables whose addictive tartness, pungency, heat, sourness and crunch I find impossible to kick.

The addictive quality is at its most powerful with gari, the wafer-thin slices of pickled ginger that are the knee-jerk accompaniment to sushi. There is always a short, squat jar in the fridge, crisp shavings of the young roots with their sparkle of salt and citrus heat, a world away from the soft beige flaps that accompany trays of commercial sushi. The purest quality is made with young, firm ginger that has the palest-pink halo round its edge, but much is coloured artificially and hardly the worse for it. (I avoid the fluorescent-pink variety, which is as sweet and garish as candy.) The cookery writer Joanna Weinberg once described sushi ginger as being 'the colour of ballet slippers'.

The real crunch comes with pickled cucumbers. Slimmer than the usual, and with fewer seeds, the Japanese variety is thinly sliced and preserved in brine, sometimes with a little rice bran or soy. They seem the most salty of the pickles, which makes them as tempting as the plain crisps to which I am devoted.

The glorious pickled-cabbage colour of shibazuke – preserved aubergine and cucumber – comes from red shiso leaves and plum vinegar. Cut into short strips and marinated with salt and vinegar, shredded red perilla leaves and ginger, this tsukemono lies at the heart and soul of what is known as Kyoto pickles and is the one I always hope to find arriving with my donburi.

I can live without yellow pickled daikon or radish – they provide a toothsome enough crunch to rice but often come with an overload of soy – and yet they somehow find their way into my shopping bag. Along with the others, they provide the crisp, clean, hot and sour notes I have an almost insane need for. Notes which, over the years, have replaced my need for the sweet and creamy. Notes that excite the palate rather than deaden it.

Don't even get me started on umeboshi ...

A dish of white-tipped radishes pickled in fresh yuzu juice.

The benign intimacy of a spoon

A spoon is naturally soft in the mouth, rounded and smooth, and with that comes a certain gentleness. There is tenderness to a spoon – the way its bowl touches my lower lip. My top lip gets to feel the liquid inside, its warmth and comfort, before even a drop is swallowed.

A spoon is hospitable, it is what I use to put food on my loved one's plate. It is the first thing a baby associates with nourishment after the breast. Its smooth edges and soft shape bring comfort. A fork, with its sharp prongs to spear the food on the plate, feels somewhat violent in comparison. Food eaten from a spoon seems more sustaining than that from a fork because it often comes surrounded by a pool of broth, sauce, soup or gravy. An extra little puddle of nourishment.

Some of my spoons are made of wood, something I warmly recommend. The sound of a wooden spoon on a wooden bowl makes your morning porridge a softly spoken start to the day. They possess a soothing quality lacking in those made of metal. That said, most of my spoons are made of stainless steel rather than silver or silver plate. The few pieces of second-hand silverware I have remain tarnished.

A spoon can do little harm. Its lack of sharp edges and points renders it safe. Unlike the knife, fork and (even) the chopstick, I doubt a spoon has ever been implicated in a murder.

The soup spoon is particularly benign. The wide, shallow bowl allows the surface of the soup to cool quickly, so my tender lips and tongue come to no harm, but is also wide enough to hold the beans and diced vegetables of a minestrone. I am somewhat saddened by its demise.

When a spoon doesn't work it is often a question of balance or, more accurately, lack of it. Sometimes the neck will be too angular or the shoulders too broad, or perhaps the bowl will be too deep and pointed, making it necessary to dip your tongue into it to extract the last morsel of custard.

To be truly comfortable in hand and mouth, the handle, neck and bowl need to be in harmony. Any spoon will do its job, and I am grateful for that. (I speak as someone who once ate a curry in his hotel room with a credit card.) But finding the right spoon, the perfect shape, weight and design, can add immeasurably to the enjoyment of what is in our bowl or on our plate. Something that designers might like to ponder before they try to reinvent this particular wheel.

Sweet Jesus
The Cyclades, Greece

The whiteness hurts. The stinging, eye-piercing white of Greek island walls, lanes and cobbles in the sun. The violent scarlet of geraniums on sky-blue windowsills. The screaming magenta of bougainvillea. It is all here, along with the relentless blue sky and the tinnitus of chirruping crickets. I long for cool, for long shadows and for the peace of soft, muted colours.

I duck into a dingy, deserted café. A whirring fan, a dog with matted fur and air that is so cold I almost wish I had a shawl with me. Separating the restaurant from the kitchen is a hotplate with battered aluminium tins, like those of school dinners, trays of luke-warm roasted peppers and deep moussaka with a wrinkled crust. Every dish seems to be settling, calming down after a morning in the oven.

On the side of the cooker, next to the hob, is a shoulder of lamb sitting sleepily in its juices. The fat is crisp and the colour of honey, so golden it is as if illuminated from inside. I walk round the counter to take a closer look. The shoulder is skinny, awkward, more bone than flesh. The fat looks even better now, and I am close enough to smell the burnt twigs of thyme in the tin. The welcome is perfunctory. I ask for a few slices of meat and a tomato salad, go back to my table and wooden school chair and give the stain-less-steel cutlery a good wipe with my T-shirt.

The salad is tomatoes, oil and salt. The fruit hacked into ungainly pieces and piled in a white dish with oil the colour of emeralds. The meat is not sliced but torn from the bone in one jagged lump. The flesh is dark pink, like a bruise, the crust deep black-brown, like old desiccated wood, chewy, almost burnt. There are hints of garlic and the ubiquitous thyme, and something magical that comes from roasting meat in a tin as old as time. A tin that is probably rarely given more than a cursory daily rinse before being used for another piece of meat. The juices are thin, salty and sticky with ribbons of black Marmite-like goo.

It is the lamb of my dreams. The meat so sweet, the juices so salty, the fat crisp in that way it so rarely is at home. This is the lamb that comes from an animal that has spent its life on a rocky hillside, eating wild oregano and scrub in blazing sunshine. It is the lamb that comes from being cooked slowly in a knackered old oven by someone who has cooked it without fuss or even care every day for most of their life. This ... is the lamb of God.

In Istanbul we eat a breakfast on the terrace, cats at our feet. On our plates a muddle of cheese. A crumbly white one labelled 'bag of goat'; 'string cheese', which is the sort of processed Cheddar you put in a schoolkid's lunchbox, and a brown version the colour of fudge labelled simply 'herbed cheese'. We trickle red-brown syrup over it from a jar labelled 'mulberry molasses'.

The blossom picnic
Fukuoka, Japan

We are armed with shopping bags and wicker baskets, bento boxes and picnic hampers, and heading for the park. Uncomfortable with crowds (there are hundreds of us), it crosses my mind to walk in the opposite direction.

Despite the numbers there is calm, as if everyone is entering a museum. Perhaps they, too, are awed by the pale-pink canopy above our heads, the carpet of blossom at our feet and the petals that fall like snowflakes as most of us sit cross-legged under the cherry trees.

The scene could be a film set. Extended families, young couples, grandmas, toddlers and tiny dogs. There are elderly ladies holding paper parasols, children with Hello Kitty backpacks and punks in leather jackets and heavy black boots. White-paper boxes of cakes with lemon icing and pink cherry blossoms appear on the grass; salmon sushi in shallow lacquered trays and triangles of snow-white onigiri wrapped in sheets of dried seaweed. Even the sugar buns from the bakers are decorated with pink blossom. Children run under the trees, laughing, chattering like water running over stones.

I have a picnic of sorts, mostly cakes. A strawberry and cream cheese sandwich, the milk bread so fluffy it is like biting into a cloud; a pair of red-bean-paste mochi and a coffee-cream choux bun. I sit and read but cannot concentrate. I eat my sweet afternoon tea and walk along the paths to the castle. The fluff of blossom is more sparse now, the flowers single rather than double and somehow more beautiful, with less pressure to perform. The stream of families thins to a trickle of lovers holding hands, taking cute photographs under the boughs.

On the way back I retrace my steps through the park, more slowly this time, exhausted from an afternoon on my feet. The crowds have dispersed, the petals still falling. There is barely an imprint in the grass. Not one wrapper, bottle or discarded bag to be seen.

The sudden notion, a yearning for something you haven't tasted for a while. Today it is long pickled chillies, the type that curl up like Aladdin's slippers, pink pickled turnips ice-cold from the fridge and jagged lumps of sharp white cheese.

Your favourite thing to eat

It is a question I feel I have been asked rather too often. 'Oh ... and one last question ... what is your favourite thing to eat?' It is almost impossible to answer truthfully, because my favourite today is unlikely to be my favourite tomorrow. The outcome of such frankly unimaginative interrogation is most likely to be the first thing that comes to mind. To date, I have always managed a gracious response, if secretly through clenched teeth.

But what *is* the answer. Are we talking sweet things (gooseberry crumble) or savoury (sashimi)? Is it a winter's day (porridge with maple syrup) or deepest summer (chilled agedashi tofu)? Is it a pre-prandial snack (plain crisps) or post-dinner tipple (umeshu with umeboshi)? Is it a snack (plain crisps again) or an indulgent treat (yuzu soft-serve in a cornet)? And what about chargrilled chicken with lemon and za'atar or roast potatoes prised from the roasting tin? What about whipped cod's roe or buttered crumpets?

The brutal answer is that my response will change according to who is doing the asking and where the answer is to be published. (Fibbing is fun.)

But sometimes telling the truth is necessary if only for one's peace of mind and, I suppose, self-respect. And so we are back to plain crisps.

In a wood in Kent I come across a wooden pole pierced with nails and on each spike is an apple, russet-skinned or flushed with crimson. An offering to the spirits of the woods perhaps. It is Halloween, and as dusk approaches the unexplained pole and its pierced apples feels faintly sinister.

Apricots, rosewater and ginger
Kochi, India

The dust from the indoor spice market has permeated my clothes, my hair, my lungs. The ghost of ground ginger and pepper, fine and soft like talcum powder. Dust, on this trip, has been the dust of fatigue, of traffic jams and T-shirts whose armpits smell of cumin. But not today. This is dust that energises and lifts the spirits, that makes my eyes tingle and my nose run. Dust that has awakened me from a torpor born of travelling long distances on the subcontinent.

Freshly ground dried ginger smells different to that which has been stored in a jar, even one that is tightly stoppered. Along with its usual dusky, dry-earth heart there are top notes of citrus too, the sort you find in fresh ginger or lime leaves but very rarely in dried. This ginger is a revelation and nothing like the dried ginger in my pot at home.

I arrive back at my lodgings to a battered-tin dish of dried apricots in syrup. Small and plump, round rather than oval, and freckled with rust. I dip a spoon into the syrup, a pretty spoon battered and bent from years of service, and sip the heavily chilled, sweet liquor. Lighter than that used to soak gulab jamun, the heavy, sticky balls of dough I have consumed with nothing short of gluttony on this trip, but thinner and less cloying and with the faintest breath of rosewater. I sit in peace on the cool veranda with my tin dish of apricots like dumpy cherubs and with the dry citrus dust of ground ginger still in my hair.

Early spring, Kamakura, and a small basket appears at my table and a tiny dish of salt. In it, a single whisp of new season's bracken in tempura batter, the fern caught in the process of slowly unfurling.

Licking the bowl

No chocolate or ginger cake, Victoria sponge or coffee and walnut cake tastes quite as good as that smudge of raw cake mixture stolen from the bowl. The beaten butter and sugar, eggs and flour have a special temptation all of their own. Cool and whipped till cloud-like, it has a hint of soft-serve vanilla ice cream about it. You can't eat much, of course, not even a full spoonful, only the merest fingertip's worth, a dab, a swoosh. But that is the point. Perhaps it is what makes raw cake mixture irresistible, the fact that it must be taken in precious amounts. Anyone who has dipped into excess knows how your treat soon cloys. We indulge at our peril.

I say 'licking the bowl', but our delight need not be confined to that. Wiping the extra uncooked cake mixture from the spoon or beater with your index finger is just as good. Seasoned with the false premise of waste not, want not, the raw mixture also carries with it the frisson of the illegal. In cookery classes at school in the late 1960s we were allowed to lick the black-treacle spoon but not the one we used for golden syrup, and certainly not one smeared with the vanilla-scented delights of raw cake mixture, so we (by which I mean me and all the girls in the class) developed a way of sneaking some with the deftness of a bunch of serial shoplifters.

There's a fat bumblebee caught in the kitchen skylight. Something that happens on an almost daily basis at the height of summer. He has spent a good ten minutes trying to get through the glass. If he lives for the usual twenty-eight days, that is two full years of his life. I rescue him with a long-handled feather duster and take him outside. There is not even the briefest nod of gratitude.

The disapproving eel lady
Tokyo

I am being watched. Her eyes are going through me like a laser, she is reading my inner thoughts. She does not approve.

On the table in front of me is a red-lacquer tray on which sits a rectangular dish, also lacquered, a work of art in deep rust-red and black, shiny as lip gloss. The position of the tray, the dish, my cup of smoky broth and dish of pickles, my chopsticks and their rest is exact, as if measured with a ruler. On a deep bed of rice sits a neat rectangle of grilled eel fillets, a dish I could easily choose as my last supper if I could eat it here, in Japan. Those bronzed pieces of fish, shiny, soft enough to cut with chopsticks and tantalisingly savoury, are the food I dream of when I am on the plane, and are now sitting in their shining box, dusted very lightly with fine green sansho pepper. What I refer to as Japanese dust – the ground dried berries with notes of pepper and citrus.

I have spent over a year of my life in this country. I understand enough about Japanese etiquette to know I am behaving correctly: my bag is on a stand, rather than the floor; I do not have my headphones on and have done all my necessary nodding and smiling. For once, too, I am quite neat and tidy. And yet still she glares. Haughty, disdainful, almost threatening. I check my buttons.

As I pay and depart we bow to one another, a half-bow, a nod of cool respect. As I leave, her lips break into a warm smile. 'Thank you for coming. So nice to see you again.'

A sea urchin in its spiky shell. Saffron-orange flesh cupped in a shell of black spines, served on a bed of green conifer leaves.

The bacon sandwich

Never for breakfast or lunch and certainly not for supper, the bacon sandwich deserves a special moment of its own. Working outside on a stone-cold day, returning home after a movie or from a trip to the pub, rashers of streaky held between two slices of white bread warm the soul like nothing else.

Streaky bacon, marbled with creamy fat on dark-maroon flesh like Florentine endpapers is my bag, but others prefer back bacon, smoked or not. If I have any rules at all, they are that a bacon sandwich should always be slightly too big, never elegant. Cutting one diagonally into triangles is unforgivable. In my kitchen it will never be cut at all. Part of the gluttonous joy of such a thing is that it is too large to eat in polite company. In my book, a bacon sandwich is a two-hands job.

Today's bacon sandwich is more of a celebration than usual. Dead of winter, but it feels like spring. The snowdrops are out and the sky is a piercing pale blue, like David Hemmings's eyes in *Blow-Up*. I have just given the zinc table in the garden its first polish of the year, a messy job involving tubs of beeswax and old dusters, but a deeply satisfying one.

I pile the bacon on one side of the frying pan, rasher upon crisp rasher, then press one slice of bread into the hot fat. Sponge-like, it sucks up the hot liquor and the odd nugget of bacon that has fallen from the rasher. I stop as soon as I can see the ghost of my fingerprints appear in fat on the surface of the bread. I regard these marks as being as crucial to the finished thing as does a potter his stamp or a painter his signature.

The joyless would no doubt suggest that grilling your bacon would be a healthier option, but that would leave us bereft of any fat in which to dip our bread. We are talking about a bacon sandwich here, so any conversation about healthy eating is pretty much a non-starter. A bacon sandwich improves my health enormously ... by which I mean my mental health. Few curries or pizzas, ice creams or puddings can boost the endorphins quite like a bacon butty on a cold day. Or any day, come to think of it.

Breakfast in a rather dingy hotel dining room, near the Roman ruins of Baalbek in eastern Lebanon. There are bowls of yoghurt; blue-and-white jugs of fresh mint, a basket of dimpled sheets of warm flatbread folded like delicate ancient manuscripts, and pots of honey and fig jam. A lone brick of stale Madeira cake sits on an oval white plate. It is labelled 'English'.

That second cup of tea

If you wriggle through the lane that runs from Hanover Square with its vast plane trees towards the shiny shops of London's Bond Street, you will find a Georgian house, painted black (it's actually very, very dark green, but let us not split hairs) with two bow windows full of hand-made teapots and tea bowls. A few days short of my fiftieth birthday, stepping into this spare, quiet room, I drank what was only the second cup of tea of my life.

My parents had made an attempt, some forty-five years earlier, to wean their small son off blackcurrant cordial, which was the only drink I would allow to pass my lips. I spat out this new brown brew with its milky notes and sugary aftertaste and never went near it again.

I had known the house in Dering Street in its previous life as an art gallery and ventured through the door, mistakenly in search of coffee. Sitting at the long oak table and too embarrassed to leave, I suggested the owner choose something for me, explaining apologetically that I liked neither milk nor sugar.

What arrived changed my life. A tall cup, no handle, blue stripes as delicate as a spider's web running down its sides, sitting on a tiny wooden saucer. The content was clear, pale green and smelled of a summer lawn just mown. It was not steaming-hot but comfortingly warm, verdant and with a piercing clarity of colour. Tea, green, bright and umami-rich, is now so much part of my life that I can hardly think of a time without it. Two, three times a day is not too often; I am making up for half a century of wasted time.

The owner, Timothy d'Offay, is now a dear friend, the person who first encouraged me to travel to Japan, who introduced me to the senchas and gyokuros, the hōjichas and oolongs that now mark the progress of each day as surely as the ticking of a clock. I will be forever grateful.

A pancake at the market
Seoul, South Korea

The roof of the market, its lights and pipes and ducts, are wrapped in tin foil. I can only assume that replacing the foil must be easier than cleaning. There are a hundred people, maybe more, sitting at communal tables, eating or waiting to eat. Few of us are over thirty.

A pale-blue bowl the size of a baby's bath is full to the brim with yellow batter, thick with shredded white onions and chopped spring onion. I fancy there is some potato in there too. A woman with John Lennon glasses and a scarlet apron pats the batter into thick cakes the size of a side plate, then lowers them into shallow oil and looks after them, tenderly turning each with the help of two metal fish slices. Once both sides are golden she lifts the cakes from the bubbling oil, stacking her handiwork in neat piles.

My pancake – thick, crisp, a luminous yellow – is cut in half and stuffed uncomfortably into a paper cup. (The woman next to me takes four wrapped in foil and carries them away in her shopping bag.) There are no spare seats, so I eat as I walk. There is as much onion as batter, the crust is rough and crisp, the inside a soft tangle of alliums that makes my lips tingle.

A green tray of seashells – whelk, clam and cockle – used as a giant ashtray outside a dumpling shack in Itaewon, South Korea. I have never seen a more beautiful collection of cigarette butts.

It is heartening when readers come up to me and tell me which of my recipes they have been making, but especially so when they include those which they make each year to celebrate some event or another. The salmon pie on Christmas Eve perhaps, or the sausage pasta with mustard and cream on their anniversary. I have often wondered why I feel such delight when this happens. It dawns on me today that it is not just that it gives me a brief sense of purpose; it is also a relief to hear that the recipes actually work.

Queuing for sheeps' heads
Tehran

My friend is being a little vague as to what we are queuing for, but I go with it. This looks like a clean, spartan café and I trust him. Meisam has yet to let me down.

There must be twenty of us in line, all men, and it is barely eight o'clock in the morning. Many of Tehran's inhabitants are returning from prayer. We reach the threshold and I peer inside. I catch the eye of the tall, unsmiling server. He whispers to his colleague and they grin conspiratorially.

On a counter just inside the door is a stainless-steel bowl piled with skinned sheeps' heads, eyes agog, and next to it a vat of clear, beige broth. Steam rises. In the broth sits another bowl of liquid; its depths are fatty and bronze, its surface shimmering with coins of bright-orange fat. Two sheeps' heads perch on the rim as if in conversation. The server mashes something grey-brown in a small bowl, then pours a ladle of broth into it, stirs it and hands it to my friend. 'It's the brain,' he says, 'a treat for your guest.'

I sit. A bowl of the broth is put on the Formica-topped table in front of me. I am instructed to add a dash of vinegar and chilli oil from the heavy glass bottles on the table. Salt too. The liquor, silky with fat and deeply savoury, heals the soul. We are given a tin plate with bits of sheep on it to nibble. I recognise the tongue but little else. I sip the hot, marrow-warming soup and politely slurp the proffered brain, telling myself I am taking my mother's mantra of 'waste not, want not' to its limit.

A café, so overgrown by climbing greenery you only know it exists by the smell of ground coffee coming from the door.

Marmalade day

The wicker basket of gnarled and dimpled bitter oranges is glowing like a beacon, the fruits flashed here and there with viridian, their skins tight to the flesh beneath. Each one sports a bright-green button, which is all that is left of its stem. The words 'Seville oranges', written in red, are as welcome as the sight of the first pink stalks of rhubarb, or lemons with their glossy leaves intact. I buy two kilos and take them home with a spring in my step – a brown paper carrier bag of sunshine on a clear and frosty January morning.

I make coffee and tear apart a cardamom sugar bun, then slice each fruit in half, scooping out the pips and pulp with a spoon as I go. Bundled up in a square of muslin, the pectin-rich innards of the fruit will sit amongst the bubbling peel, ensuring a fine, soft set to the jam.

I take my sharpest knife, a small paring knife with a blade like a razor, and slice the empty orange shells into the thinnest strips I can manage, each one a half-moon of orange zest and thick white pith. They go into my deepest saucepan with two and a half litres of water and a pinch of salt, then I bring them to the boil. The heat lowered, they are simmered at a languid bubble for a couple of hours.

I test a slice of orange every now and again, looking for peel that is now translucent and soft to the bite. It takes two full hours. The mixture cools and then I tip the sloppy, golden fruit and juice into a stainless-steel bowl and let it sleep overnight in the fridge to extract every possible gram of pectin, the fruits' natural setting agent.

Next morning, the sky clear and white, I bubble up the oranges with sugar (one cup of pulp to one cup of sugar) and let them simmer for about twenty-five minutes. The brass thermometer says 105°C, but I still test the old-fashioned way, a habit that is unlikely to change till I die, by dropping a teaspoon of the preserve onto a fridge-cold saucer. I try this three times, five minutes' simmering between each attempt, until the syrup begins to move slowly on the saucer, as if tethered in place. It does not instantly set, but I can tell it isn't far off.

Off the hob, the orange jam is left to settle for a few minutes, then stirred and ladled into glass jars. Four pots of glistening amber, the curls of peel suspended like jewels in the deep-orange jelly. The kitchen is still cold, and with the scent of oranges and syrup in the air I feel the urge to make a rack of toast.

Marmalade is always a pot of joy. Button-bright, glistening and quivering on the spoon, it has none of the cloying sweetness of honey, a clarion call to the start of the day. Whisper it: this thick orange jam does not feel quite right at any other time of day. It glows like a candle on the greyest January morning, cheering us out of the door to work. No preserve causes such controversy, thick-cut or hair-thin, dark or pale, softly set or firm. Mine will be barely set, light in colour and as much golden jelly as peel.

Any morning now, the garden white with frost, I will pick up one of the jars I have filled today, twist off the glossy black lid and inhale. I will dip in my spoon, spread the lumpy jam onto a piece of hot toast, wipe a bittersweet tear of syrup from the crust and start my day.

Dumplings in an alley
Seoul, South Korea

At the far end of the alleyway, clouds of steam billow like breath from a dragon. I walk over cigarette ends and past dead plants and duck under grubby washing, wincing at the sinister-smelling doorways and puddles of what I very much doubt is rainwater.

As I get closer, snatches of white move amongst the steam and then a face appears, plump as a pumpkin. The chef squints at me through the clouds and we both smile. He is lifting the lids of bamboo baskets stacked four high, checking the chubby white buns within – fat mandu stuffed with minced pork and shredded cabbage, chives and glass noodles – shaped like half-moons or the hats of trainee chefs. He tends his parcels slowly, deliberately, not a single movement wasted, every now and again entirely hidden by steam. As each tray of dumplings becomes ready, he shouts and passes it through the open window into the restaurant behind.

I step inside. No one greets or even notices me, save a female chef in a white dumpling hat who nods sternly as if to say, 'Don't worry, we've clocked you.' All the diners have their coats and hats on. I take one of the mismatched stools at the counter next to some heavy tins of cooking oil and fiddle with the short plastic bottles of soy and what I assume is vinegar. I play with the tumbler of metal chopsticks and deep-bowled spoons and tug a tissue from the wooden dispenser. I would help myself to a paper cup of water from the machine but there is a table blocking my way. I look at my phone, then the posters hanging from the ceiling on a string, which I assume are the menus. I think I am being ignored.

Suddenly, a waitress hands me a laminated menu and stands there whilst I take it all in. Her body language is impatient, her smile tight. I point at several of the pictures and smile. She doesn't. Minutes later she returns from the open kitchen at the end of the restaurant with two brown plates of steamed jjin mandu on a paper napkin, the fat pockets of dough stuffed to bursting with shrimp and chives, and a plate of untidy crisp pork dumplings that I would be happy to live on for the rest of my life. There is a tiny plastic dish of soy and another of orange kimchi and a deep black bowl of soup with shredded omelette and spring onions floating to the surface. I pour the sticky soy into a little white dipping dish and add a few drops of the dark vinegar. My dumplings, doughy, spicy, scorching-hot and as comforting as an old teddy bear, are gone in a heartbeat.

Five minutes later, I call the waitress over and order more. She nods ... she knows.

Snow-white crab meat in an individual bamboo steamer. I lift the lid and inhale the sea.

Eating roses
Lebanon

We are batting away the pesky wasps that have come to take a dip in the jams – apricot, fig, mulberry, rose – that sit shimmering in pressed-glass dishes in the sunshine. We sit in the shade of a mulberry tree overlooking a field of damask rose bushes and sumac trees. There is a brief moment of drama when a spider the size of a drone makes a run for the door that leads to the kitchen with its vats of simmering orange preserve. He is brutally despatched with a perfectly aimed broom.

I have come to pick roses for a film, but the sun is too bright to shoot or to pick, so we do neither. The petals are usually gathered early in the day, after the dew has dried and when they are just warm from the early-morning sun. We mock-up a shot with a wicker basket full to the brim with blousy, deep-pink blooms whose fragrance could reach you, on a light breeze, from twenty feet away.

My lesson on which blooms to pick and how to do so to preserve their scent is followed by lunch on the stone terrace. We eat flatbreads, warm and patchily charred from the griddle, folded over crumbled white cheese, tearing them apart and dipping the smoky bread and salty cheese into bowls of rose-scented jam.

There are three climbing roses in my own garden. Pink and buff Souvenir de Madame Léonie Viennot scurries up the back of the house, a rambler without a map; Souvenir de Docteur Jamain, the crimson-black of a blood clot, seeps into the medlar tree whilst Direktör Benschop, also known as City of York, climbs the taller of the two yew hedges, then, in late June, cascades down the sides. A small avalanche of creamy-white petals.

Madame Viennot was first bred in 1858 in Lyons by the rose breeder Jean-Alexandre Bernaix and named for his wife. She needs a firm hand with the secateurs each winter. Docteur Jamain is a bit of an old fusspot and capricious to boot, but has a truly divine fragrance. This is the rose you need for rose petal jam, though I have yet to make a single pot. Bred by François Lacharme, it was introduced in 1865, three years after the doctor's passing. Direktör Benschop is a semi-double milky-white rose with egg-yolk-yellow stamens bred by German breeder Mateus Tantau in 1939, though not commercially available till after the war. The garden is also home to Alchymist, the crumpled honey, white and gold climber.

I have always struggled with the notion of stripping a rose for its petals, though I do occasionally bring one into the kitchen in June, scattering them over an oval platter of raspberries, a sponge cake dusted with icing sugar or, most memorably, a vast fig meringue the size of a hat at a June wedding.

Eating rosewater ice cream from a shop in Beirut whose walls are riddled with bullet holes.

Hōjicha
Hokkaido, Japan

I can smell breakfast as I shuffle along the corridor in the hotel's oversized slippers. The greeting is that of steaming rice, tofu and roasted tea. There is also sweet potato in a small dish of dashi. I am happy but long for coffee. My request is politely refused. This is not unusual. The more ancient and isolated the inn, the less likely they are to have coffee at breakfast. If you are staying more than one night, it may turn up the following day, though it is unlikely to be the tiny cup of heart-starter you crave.

The liquid in my cup is more likely to be green than brown. The exception is hōjicha, the roasted green tea that I associate with breakfast in Japan, despite it having a somewhat brown and 'sleepy' character. Maybe that is its tendency to offer less caffeine. Today I have little choice but to start my day this way.

The sweet, almost smoky hōjicha carries a hint of toast, especially in the darker roasted varieties. The leaves are often the colour of tobacco. If I was ever to give up coffee – a somewhat unlikely event, I admit – it is this with which I would start my day. Often a mixture of both leaves and twigs, it is occasionally mixed with roasted rice, offering a smell that is both ancient and deeply comforting.

Sometime around ten, I will now often stop work to make hōjicha. A single cup, maybe two. I take it unusually weak. Whilst it is often made with an entire tablespoon of roasted leaves per pot, I use just a teaspoon. Simpler to make and more instantly calming than most green teas, you can use just-off-the-boil water rather

58

than wait for your kettle to cool, as you must with most green teas; 80ºC is about right if your brew is not to be bitter, and it can be steeped for as little as thirty seconds. Though don't drink it just yet. You will burn your lips. Let it cool awhile in your cup. I usually make a second infusion, when I let the leaves and water stay in each other's company for a full minute.

A train, going through hills and woods in Kyushu, whose seats face outwards so you can admire the view. I have had enough of tempura, sashimi, tofu and bean curd. I go to a little café in the backstreet that serves faintly European food. I eat something called old-fashioned cake, which turns out to be a thick slice from a tray-bake, the fat, buttery cake crumbs stuffed with blackcurrants. A ball of vanilla ice cream on the side.

A sense of place
Ammiq, Beqaa, Lebanon

Lunch in the Beqaa Valley. Rocks the colour of rolled oats. Pathways of bleached sand winding through knee-high dried grasses. Crisp seed heads rattle like snakes. Here and there a green bush of olive or sumac stands unbowed against the unrelenting sun. Rows of clipped thyme bushes neat as a pin guide us towards the restaurant.

Twenty or more tables are sheltered by a vast canopy of wide, slatted straw that covers the chairs, floor and diners with prisms of piercing golden light. Other tables sit in the shade of mulberry trees bent towards the sun. Inside, sheltered from the blinding rays, is a vast buffet. Long steel tables hold white platters of local dishes: geometrically arranged falafel; creamy, deeply smoky moutabal; clouds of white labneh dusted with red sumac and slivered almonds; the obligatory hummus with pools of green oil and strips of white baladieh cheese with olives and fresh wild thyme. Roast potatoes have been rolled in a dressing of garlic and chopped herbs; a bowl of yoghurt has a wreath of dried mint. There are sticky date pastries cut into diamonds and a silver bowl of purple plums.

We sit on the terrace, a little bit of everything on our white plates. A lunch steeped in olives and olive oil, thyme, sumac, smoke, mint and za'atar. The very essence of the parched landscape in which we sit.

Making walnut pastries in Beirut, pressing them into pretty wooden moulds, ready to bake. Walnut-coloured, they resemble lumps of plaster moulding, like a Victorian ceiling cornice, or perhaps chess pieces.

The hot cross bun

When you split and toast a hot cross bun, the warmth releases the smell of cinnamon and the citrus oils in the candied peel. The bun should be torn part, never cut. Teasing one half from the other with your fingers provides a craggy surface whose furrows will hold the melted butter in tiny puddles like rain on a hoggin path.

But (and it is a big but) the rough, toasted surface is never quite hot enough to melt the butter. Once the buttering is done, something that is to be set about with extreme generosity, the bun must be placed back under the grill in order for the butter to melt.

Perfection is when you manage to catch the bun just as the butter has formed a golden pool yet retains a patch of glistening, soft-but-not-yet-liquid butter at its centre. A shining, golden coin in the middle of your bun.

If you take it slowly, concentrating on your every movement, cooking can be a deeply meditative experience. Rush it, and it becomes purely about the end result, about sustenance.

Morning greens

Food can delight, astound, amuse and sustain. It can appease, invigorate, intrigue or console. Food also has the possibility to take us back to basics.

In times of overload and confusion, when there are too many things demanding my attention, like today, I make a bowl of greens. A pot of water at a rolling boil, I rain in a handful of young broccoli – the sort with long, crisp, emerald stems – and let it bubble for barely two minutes. I lift out the stalks and plunge them immediately into a bowl of cold water and jangling ice cubes to stop them cooking. The freezing water sets their colour. They are then shaken dry and piled in an unadorned bowl.

I scatter over them a handful of sprouting seeds – green and white mung, purple radish and tiny, pale freckles of broccoli sprouts from the chiller in the health food store. A handful of diminutive leaves, the palest-yellow heart leaves of a little gem lettuce; curling wisps of pea shoots or sprigs of dark-green watercress are introduced and a shake of citrus soy from the tall bottle in the fridge.

I eat my big green bowl of salad with chopsticks. The broccoli and leaves are easy to negotiate, but the seeds are more difficult. That is the point. I am taken back to basics by the idea of new shoots and unfurling leaves, the wonder of a seed coming to life. Trying to pick up a sprouted mung bean with chopsticks is a task that makes you grateful for every mouthful. A bowl of youth and green shoots to restore a state of equilibrium.

Turning over a roast chicken in its roasting tin and squirrelling out the two oysters of flesh behind the leg, like plump little cushions.

Oden, and football at the counter
Tokyo

My hotel is not where I expected. The area turns out to be noisy, the shops loud and crowded, the street dirty and lined with young women dressed as cats, bunny rabbits and dolls handing out flyers. I walk hopefully, desperately looking for something to eat that isn't fried or served in a bun. About to give up and return defeated to my room, I take a short cut through the dark piss-alleys off the main street.

A single scarlet lantern hangs from a doorway, a wooden umbrella stand with room for twelve lies empty. Inside a kitchen brigade is busy at work, but the sign says 'closed'. It is eight-thirty in the evening. Two young businessmen stand outside, clearly mystified. One gingerly slides open the wooden door whose old glass rattles in its frame and says a few words to what appears to be the owner. She laughs, then they laugh and she ushers us all in, slightly embarrassed. She turns the 'closed' sign to 'open'.

I order a beer and ponder the laminated menu. What intrigues is not so much the 'tube-shaped fishcake', 'fried yam cake' or the 'mashed tofu with lotus and burdock root', but the long (and slightly sinister) water bath behind the counter, its wooden lid issuing intermittent puffs of steam like the hot springs at Beppu. She lifts the lid to reveal simmering lumps of meat and sliced radish, boiled eggs and dumplings within. It reminds me of Liverpudlian scouse.

Avoiding the egg at my request, the owner ladles the anonymous meat, roots and clear brown broth into a deep bowl and sets it down in front of me. The diminutive size of my room, the screaming neon horror of the area fades away with one sip of hot soup and a chunk of boiled beef. Oden is many things: a stew of fishcakes and radish, boiled eggs and root vegetables or bits of meat that need a long, slow cooking. Winter food that is both cheap and nourishing, though little more. But to me, right now, it is the most comforting thing that has ever passed my lips.

I watch the football on the small television screen behind the bar. I have no idea who is playing, neither do I care. I watch as I always do, for the football, caring little about goals or who is winning. (Though I might feel differently if it was my team playing.) The programme is interrupted every few minutes by those shouty neon-coloured adverts with a half-animated, half-hysterically jabbering male presenter that leave you thinking someone has slipped something into your beer.

A restaurant is somewhere to eat, to drink, to be amongst friends. Sometimes it is simply a sanctuary, a place safe from the world outside.

Midnight. Hokkaido. I climb out of the uncomfortably hot outdoor cedar bath and roll in the deep snow.

A hymn to plain crisps

We are sitting in the panelled bar of an ageing 'grande-dame' hotel in Mayfair. A cocktail or two with James after a long and blissful lunch elsewhere to celebrate my OBE. The waiter brings crisps. Actually, not crisps but game chips, fried on the premises. Light, crisp and as fragile as a butterfly's wing, they are addictive and we demolish bowl after bowl.

Whenever the subject of favourite crisps comes up, as it so often does, everyone present seems a bit sniffy when I tell them that my preferred crisps are the cheap, ready-salted variety. As a teenager, little could beat the rasp of cheese and onion or the sting of salt and vinegar, but as the years go by I find those flavours too strong.

Nothing anyone can do to a crisp can push the mundane ready-salted from its pedestal. No pickled onion, wasabi or olive flavour will ever outflank it. The wafer-thin Spanish potato crisps fried in olive oil are gorgeous if you are only eating a few with a drink, but too rich and oily to wolf in quantity. The Italian brands are not quite salty enough. Posh British brands are too thick or too greasy. No, for me it must be the everyday plain crisps that can be picked up in any newsagent's. It is the one time commerce gets things totally right. Please don't @ me.

Opening the fridge first thing in the morning to find a bowl of chilled rice pudding. I eat it just as it is, no jam, no fruit, no treacle. Just a deep bowl of cold, creamy rice.

Lunch in the canteen
Kochi, India

Lunch in the canteen comes on a banana leaf the size of a Victorian meat platter. A pile of soft white rice, slightly wet and hollowed out like an upturned palm, holds a curry of pumpkin. Brick-red with chilli and ginger, earthy from turmeric and slightly sweet, it fizzes and tingles on my lips. The portion is modest and accompanied by pickles that are sweet and jam-like and taste of gooseberries. There is a loose pile of avial too, the okra, yam and green bean stew cooked with coconut.

We scoop up our lunch with jagged pieces of phulka, pale scorched dough puffed like newly plumped cushions.

A second dish is sharp and clean on the tongue. A pale-yellow kalan curry of raw bananas and coconut, sour with buttermilk and hot with yellow mustard seeds. Accompanied by a mound of green mango pickle, it is too liquid to pick up with the flatbread, so I ladle it into some of the rice and use my spoon.

Most of the workers are eating their lunch from battered aluminium trays, each of its neat pockets filled with thick coconut avial, pickle or kalan. A guest, I get this verdant banana leaf instead. Perhaps they assume I will Instagram it.

We tuck into dessert, a vermicelli milk pudding in a dented tin dish. Slippery and scented with cardamom with a scattering of chopped pistachios on its surface, its icy chill is welcome. The fan above our heads moves at the speed of treacle. Replete and blissfully happy, it is all I can do to stop falling asleep.

A feast of snow crab
Kinosaki, Japan

Late January, northern Kyushu. I must be on the sixth course of a
snow crab dinner. A young lady in a pale-gold kimono brings me
dish after dish, each one a glistening jewel. A single, shelled claw of
crab sashimi; a shimmering pool of dashi with a floating island of
crab meat as white as frost and a single piece of sushi with sweet,
pink leg meat. She enters my room once again with a small, heavy
wood-and-copper box that from its scars and patina could be a
hundred years old, lined with white fireproof clay. The box is filled
with ash and glowing coals.

She places it on a tray on the floor and kneels before it, lays an
empty crab shell on a wire rack set over the heat and spoons white
crab meat into it and thick, jade-green-and-grey slime – parts of the
crab's guts. This tomalley, often referred to as 'kani miso', is so
often thrown away by squeamish cooks, including this one.

The mixture is bubbling now, stirred continuously with a single
thick chopstick, the host laughing as she does so. A splash of sake
goes in, then with another blip and fizz the room fills with steam, a
smell that is part ozone, part alcohol, part sweet, rich seafood.

The crab shell and its sloppy lichen-coloured contents is placed
on the low lacquered table before me and I eat it from the hot shell.
You will either think of this as a treat beyond all treats, a gift from
the gods or something from *The Exorcist*.

Grilled mackerel, charred on the edges, on a small oval plate with a long pink shoot of pickled ginger and a snowdrift of grated radish.

Shawarma under the carob tree
Beirut, Lebanon

At the end of the lane is a cluster of assorted chairs under the branches of a carob tree. Grateful of shelter from the cracked roads and searing late-summer heat, I peel back the white paper that has kept my shawarma warm and sit. I shut out the noise, the car horns, the loud voices that surround me. Police sirens tug at my attention.

The bread is thin, like a pancake, and still warm. The stuffing is generous and I use both hands, holding the roll so tightly the filling oozes up and onto my lips. I don't miss a nugget of the crisp cauliflower, its florets browned by the grill, or a drop of the ivory sauce, the result of mixing ground walnuts with tahini, garlic and much lemon. Around me, under the tree, there is chatter but I hear little.

For five short minutes I forget the dust that coats my boots, the overflowing garbage bins and polluted air of the beautiful, broken city that is Beirut. I applaud the women who must hold up the banks with guns to get their (own) money out, those who feed the lost and homeless and those who take care of the city's stray cats. All I can think about is there in my hand and on my lips.

Fish soup
Reykjavík, Iceland

The shed lies by the boatyard, its wooden walls needing a lick of paint. Inside, the room is half panelled with tongue and groove, chipped and scratched where hungry folk have squeezed into their seats at the long wooden table. Above are paintings and prints, press cuttings and portraits, framed and hung for all to admire. We wait for our soup. Sleet crashes against the windows. The narrow room is warm, jolly with travellers and fishermen, but beware anyone who fails to close the door behind them and lets in the fearsome Iceland squall.

There is pickled herring and good brown bread but the point is the soup. It arrives in deep cups, a cheering orange-red, its surface a myriad of tiny specks of oil. This is a soup made from bones, fins and claws, a broth that gets its silken texture from the sticky cartilage of cod cheeks, its colour from crushed crab shells and its depth from fish heads.

The first spoonful stings my lips, already sore from the buffeting salt air, and I put my spoon down and wait, scanning the faded photographs of fishermen and their boats long gone. I resume; it's still too hot, but I'm cold and hungry and keen to savour layer upon piscine layer of flavour. Here is a backbone of onions and thyme, a deep, almost fruity sweetness and luxurious notes of crustacea. Here is the essence of the catch, the shells and claws and skeletons, the fins and gills and tails, all simmered to a deep rust-red liquor.

If ever there was a soup with a sense of place, it is this.

In Warsaw, the waiter brings a jug of water to the table. A glass jug that contains ice, herbs and wildflowers, pieces of cucumber and slices of orange. It is the most refreshing water I have ever had.

Morning yoghurt. Steadying the ship

In Turkey, in an old hotel that smells of decaying wood, with dusty curtains and a dark dining room as silent as a morgue, I am offered two bowls of yoghurt, one thin and lumpy, as sharp as lemon juice, and another thick, strained to the texture of clotted cream.

Minamioguni, Kyushu, and my morning yoghurt is mild, barely acidic at all. This gentle, hand-made ferment is served in a plain glass bowl, thin as ice, a single comma of dark berry purée floating on its surface.

Viili is also how I start the day in Finland, a deep snowy bowlful with a tumble of berries and their purple juices. And that juice is something with which I carefully marble my Finnish yoghurt.

Yoghurt has nursed me back to health in Goa and Delhi, stirred peacefully into warm rice. Its calming notes have settled me when agitated or nervous, brought me back down to earth after too much fancy food and set me to rights after a trauma. Just as some turn to pasta or chocolate or alcohol, I steady my own ship with yoghurt. It has been the first and last thing I have eaten for as long as I can remember. A spike of acidity to wake me as well as a settling spoonful before I climb the stairs.

I join a queue
Hakata

I am perched, a little uncomfortably, at a short, busy counter in Hakata. It is not the cleanest, and certainly not the tidiest, place in which I have eaten, but the queue was long and excitable and so I joined it. It is a myth that somewhere must be good if there is a queue outside; it often simply means it is new and the latest bait for influencers regardless of what is on your plate, but in this case my/their hunch was right.

A little lower than the counter on which I sit with my second tiny beer (my first was gone in a single gulp) is a ten-burner hob, caked in years of burnt oil. The owner, in a yellow track top and orange baseball hat, wears his belly like a trophy. It seems we are here for gyoza and little else.

A black iron dish, so hot it comes on a wooden stand with a stern warning not to touch, the ten podgy dumplings, plump with ground pork and held together by a crisp spider's web of fried cornflour, stare back at me, chuckling. Thank you for queuing for us, they seem to be saying. They are gone almost as quickly as that first beer, my mouth tingling from the heat. I repeat my order but am in and out in the space of fifteen minutes, as indeed is everyone else.

The paper-thin milk chocolate of an Easter egg.

Crumbs

I surreptitiously lick my finger and dab at the stray crumbs on my plate. Soft, fat nuggets of dark ginger cake. A tiny smudge of lemon icing. Then I run my damp finger round the plate, clockwise, a final circular motion, gathering up the last stray freckles of brown spice cake.

There isn't a crumb I don't like. The shattered crust of a baguette; the rounded pink and yellow remains of a slice of birthday sponge; the last currant from an Eccles cake or flake of puff pastry from a sausage roll. There are the spongy, butter-coated crumbs from a crumpet; a lost nib of candied peel from a hot cross bun or the sugary rubble that lies at the bottom of a dish of apple crumble. The truth is that all crumbs are good.

Not all the best crumbs are sweet, mind you. The crisp, frilly bits of batter from fried fish rescued from their paper were a childhood treat, and now I feel much the same about the swirls and swashes I make on the plate with bits of fat, waxy-fleshed sourdough and the last spots of olive oil.

I am unsure whether picking up crumbs is an act of waste not or gluttony, but I nevertheless perform the act discreetly. As a cook, seeing someone wipe up every last grain from their plate is heart-warming. As an eater, I think of it as a matter of housekeeping. (Other cultures might differ here, assuming that I am suggesting I need more.)

Crumbs are precious. The last, minuscule fragments of cake or cookie or toast. Diminutive but not insignificant. How anyone can leave them on the plate is beyond me. Mopping the final vestiges of cake with a damp finger and bringing them gently to the lips is as important to me as was the first forkful. It brings with it a sense of closure, a sign of affection. A show of gratitude.

A little cake in a sandwich shop in Kyoto. A single, bright-pink cherry blossom trapped in the snow-white icing.

A bowl of soup for breakfast
Kamakura, Japan

My first night in a ryokan. A long, low wooden inn that smells of second-hand books, toasted rice and woodsmoke. The garden is charming and unkempt. There is moss on the rocks and lichen on the trees. A stream runs past the dining room windows.

At breakfast, a worn black lacquer bowl is brought to my table. I lift the lid by its circular handle – the handle that doubles as a stand when you turn the lid upside down on your tray – then, as the steam rises first in a cloud, later in a slow, steady trail like smoke from a candle, I breathe in. A salty, mushroomy smell, as savoury as Marmite. I cradle the bowl with both hands and tip it towards my lips.

The broth – clear, glossy mahogany with swirling clouds of miso – startles. The first sip seems shockingly salty, the second somehow sweeter and milder. I keep sipping, on and on, till I arrive at the bottom of the bowl – the last few drops sandy from undissolved miso paste and with it a single slippery strip of kelp.

That bowl was the start of what has become an almost daily ritual of miso soup. I should admit straight away that I am as happy with miso soup from a silver packet of powder as with that I have mixed myself from miso paste and dashi broth. But then, so are the Japanese. The result, however, is never, ever as satisfying as that made by a Japanese cook, in Japan. I am told this is because European water is hard from calcium and magnesium deposits, whereas Japanese water is soft and its low mineral composition is better for making soup.

Miso soup sets me up for the day as surely as a bowl of porridge, though I have been known to take both. In Kanagawa or Kyoto, Okinawa or Sapporo, that soup may be made with dashi – a delicate broth of smoked dried fish and seaweed – and miso, a light (shiro) or red (aka) paste of fermented soybeans. Shiro miso has the colour of thick heather honey or fudge, is lightly salty and makes for easy drinking. Aka miso is red-brown, more savoury and umami-rich than the white, and makes, to my mind at least, a more soulful, almost melancholy broth.

Sometimes there are shreds of seaweed or a few tiny clams waiting at the bottom of your bowl, like treasure. Soup – clear, aromatic and lightly salty – is a gentle way to begin the day. I am lulled, sip by slow sip, back into the rhythm of life. I start my day in good heart.

An old wooden restaurant table in Kyushu. Odd chairs. A silver knife and fork rest on a twig. A small wooden soup spoon carved from a thin branch. A lump of green moss on which sits a tiny citrus fruit on its stem, one shiny leaf attached.

Cha
Thekkady, Kerala

In the depths of an arid field of mangolds, the soil as brown and cracked as a gingernut. The vegetables, curling like snakes, are ripening in the scorching sun. Their leaves have turned the brown of an old newspaper. Across the field, stepping between them, a young man brings us sweet milky tea in a tin flask. Everyone takes a cup gratefully whilst I politely decline. I cannot drink milky tea. This kindly man clearly cannot comprehend the idea of anyone not drinking tea. I am at once to be treated with suspicion.

A coffee house in Seoul. A line of six cone filters, with customers' choice of coffee dripping slowly through. I could be here a while.

Eating alone

It is a rare and strangely joyous thing to eat on your own. No conversation with a loved one. No music or laughter. A meal without the hubbub of life, the chatter of children or the contented hum of a restaurant at lunch. A meal all to oneself.

From time to time, I eat alone in my hotel room or in the stone-floored cellar kitchen at home. Food eaten in quiet and solitude feels like a luxury, an indulgence, and curiously illicit. Not the food of a secret eater, of shame or gluttony, but a meal of self-respect and showing yourself you need no one else in order to have a good time.

Few lines in a book have infuriated me more than the one by a writer of books about 'healthy eating' who insinuated that if you find yourself drinking alone then you may have a drink problem. Oh, do fuck off and get a life. A glass of wine on your own, like tucking into dinner by yourself, is as life-enriching as one shared with friends.

On our own hibachi, my friend Takahiro and I grill whole tiny fish at the counter and dip them into saucers of soy whilst the chef slices scallops for us to eat raw.

The peach

Late July. Friends arrive bearing gifts. A shallow white cardboard box turns out to be carrying a cluster of flat white peaches, their soft pink cheeks nudging one another. The scent of roses teases as I open the lid. Eight plump navels, their parchment skin flushed with brushstrokes of rose and carmine. I offer them around but am told they are for me alone, to enjoy when everyone has gone.

It has taken a long time to accept the flat peach. Initially I thought of it as an imposter, a peach you must nibble rather than bite. A child's peach. I cannot call them 'doughnut' as do some, an ugly name for a fruit as cute as a belly button. For me the name is Saturn, dumpling or just plain 'flat'. What they have is neatness – they will fit into a lunch or bento box – and their size allows you to eat even the ripest with a certain elegance.

True peaches, round, the size of a tennis ball, are for eating with a plate and a knife, each fruit first sliced in half, the stone prised from the flesh, then cut into quarters. You can eat such a fruit politely. But that is not the way I like to eat this fruit. A peach, in my book at least, is something to be devoured.

I want to feel the fuzz of the skin against my lips, the first bead of juice touch my bottom lip and then my tongue. The first bite that sends a single rivulet of juice down my chin and deep into my stubble. I want to suck and slurp and smack my lips, to feel the ripe flesh first on my tongue, then in my throat. If the juice drips onto my shirt or runs down my arms, then so be it.

No matter its shape or its size, the perfect peach is the most heavily scented, the softest-fleshed, the one with the sweetest, most rampant juice. No acidity needed here, like with the perfect apricot. Just the softest, most suede-like skin, the most giving flesh and the sweetest juice. That is the peach I want.

Valentine's Day, Tokyo. Strawberries, each fruit individually wrapped in cellophane, then cradled in a little protective polystyrene cape. Each one bears a sticker of its provenance. The price is the equivalent of four pounds sterling. Whilst we may have reached the pinnacle of overpackaging, they serve a purpose. You unwrap your single fruit slowly; the fragrance trapped inside the cellophane is extraordinary, the very essence of ripe berries. Each fruit has been chosen for its perfection, and against all my predictions the flavour is beyond any that I have tasted before. But I'm getting ahead of myself. These berries aren't destined for a bowl, to be eaten with sugar and cream. It is St Valentine's Day, after all.

Breakfast in Japan: 1
A cheap provincial hotel breakfast

My room is so small I must put my suitcase on the bed in order to open it. If I stretch out my arms I can touch both walls at once. Laughably labelled as a double, I imagine the dance that would ensue should you both wish to move around in this room at the same time. My fellow guests are young Japanese travellers, a few businessmen, and what looks like a visiting football team. After sharing a morning bath with said football team I pad downstairs. Such hotels allow you to eat in your pyjamas, a ritual I heartily endorse. (Even the lowliest accommodation here comes with new toothbrushes, doll's house tubes of toothpaste and soft, much-worn and washed nightwear.)

The early-morning food is both perfunctory and delicious. Wedges of grapefruit and orange, a glass of blood orange juice and a bowl of rice threaded through with flakes of dried seaweed and beads of salmon roe as bright as Christmas baubles. It is the bowl of soup that is extraordinary. The usual light, instant miso has been replaced by a rich chicken broth, deeply savoury, the beads of fat on its surface supporting a single floating mushroom.

When I am eating eel donburi from a rust-red lacquered bowl and they bring me a cup of eel broth to go with it. Deeply smoky, slightly oily, dark as night.

Breakfast in Japan: 2
A Japanese country breakfast

A winter's morning and I am first to the dining room. Risking cramp, I slide my legs under the wide rectangular table only to find a deep heated hollow as warm as a hot-water bottle in which to put my feet. Roasted tea appears, a tall cup the colour of sand, the tea a glowing red-brown. I nestle it in both hands and sip.

What follows is extraordinary in that each dish feels new, a step away from the Japanese breakfasts I am used to. Tempura of orange pumpkin brought still crackling from the kitchen; slices of yellow-tail sashimi in a puddle of sesame sauce; grilled bamboo shoots on a wooden skewer and a dish of rice porridge. There is grilled cod's roe with a pin's point of fresh wasabi, pickled butterbur buds and the earliest fiddlehead fern, simmered in dashi broth and curled up like a caterpillar. A pale-blue dish is filled with mustard greens and ground sesame.

As the light lifts, the room fills with weak and watery sunshine and I am brought a bowl of suitably pale miso broth with matchsticks of dried nori and balls of chewy white mochi. As I lay down my chopsticks a pudding appears of green-tea blancmange with two rust-red goji berries. Dessert for breakfast is something I can get on top of.

Breakfast in Japan: 3
The mother of them all

A wedge of autumn melon the colour of apricots with a honeyed scent you catch from three feet away.

A shallow lacquered tray of rust red, laid with eight individual dishes. Yoghurt in a thin glass dish; a single teardrop of deep-red syrup and a tiny green leaf float on its surface.

A deep-black raku bowl of okayu, the soft and soupy rice to gently lull us out of sleep.

A triangular dish of pickled vegetables and a single umeboshi plum.

A white bowl of chilled black hijiki seaweed and soybeans.

A pretty dish painted with wisteria flowers of the softest, stickiest silken tofu the colour of the pages of an old book, decorated with a single yellow chrysanthemum flower and a lump of fresh wasabi the size of a pea.

A single grilled flatfish on a rectangular plate barely the size of my palm, its edges crisp and toffee-coloured, its flesh white like sole. It sits on a sprig of fern, unadorned and barely seasoned. There is less than three mouthfuls of flesh. We debate the variety and settle on 'local'.

A blue-and-white bowl of neatly stacked simmered greens in ponzu sauce, on which I pounce whilst working out what might be in the adjacent oval hand-made bowl (it turns out to be a tangle of shirasu, boiled infant sardines barely a centimetre in size, to add to my rice).

The silent lady who has brought me this feast reappears with a bowl of steaming dashi with spinach and coriander sprigs and a single block of simmering tofu. This is breakfast to bring you gently back from deep, peaceful sleep. Not a dazzling citrus wake-up call, an alarm clock in edible form, but a breakfast to heal and cosset.

I sit on a pale-blue zabuton in the half-light of an early-winter morning in my grey-and-white yukata and slightly-too-large padded slippers, my legs stretched under the table. Just as I am about to leave she brings me a cup of roasted green tea in a tiny bowl, clear and bright. I gaze out at the snow starting to fall outside. Kill me now.

Rust-pink fish roe wrapped in a shiso leaf and fried in tempura batter. The fact that it is eaten in a plastic hut outdoors in January only adds to its deliciousness.

Mopping my plate

I come from a generation that insisted you could not leave the table until you had finished everything on your plate. An unhealthy and ridiculous notion now, but whose reasoning was from a time when food had until recently been rationed and in short supply and every morsel was precious. To this day I mop my plate, though probably more out of appreciation than social conscience.

I push the bread around my plate, leaving swirls and swooshes of cream and rust, like a Howard Hodgkin painting. Every droplet and puddle is sponged up by the dough, every pool and rivulet caught in the soft, white crumb. A baguette is best, its slightly burnt, crisp crust keeping my fingers dry.

Bread is preferable to any sauce spoon, even in the poshest of restaurants. It may raise a snooty eyebrow or two, but dough will always get my vote over the cold-hearted silverware. I have mopped my plate since I was a boy. I doubt that happens much nowadays. Perhaps it should.

Thin sheets of warm roti and mana'eesh are best for scooping food from plate to mouth like tactile, edible cutlery, but bread is better for sponging up the delicious detritus from the plate. The soft, open crumb swells with cream or curry sauce, gravy or meat juices, to leave us replete. A Chinese host may take a mopped plate as a sign that more food is needed, yet I would rather think of each painterly flourish as a signature, a thank-you note to the cook.

An old man with a white beard and a long scarf sits at a communal table in a café in Kyoto, drinking red wine. He is wearing a bowler hat.

A table in the sun

A vine has coiled itself round the faded posts of the pergola and across the rafters, giving us the gift of shade. There is clematis too, each flower's six swan-white petals set round a green and mauve eye. Climbing roses have made their way up the three other posts, the soft pink of Blush Noisette tangling with the vine.

Odd chairs and a long, cushioned bench run down the full length of the table, itself covered with an old white cloth embroidered with dark-purple wisteria. Dotted amongst the ice-blue tumblers and assorted vintage cutlery are single Gertrude Jekyll roses in glass jars and tall stems of deep-pink Japanese anemones. A battered Moroccan lantern hangs from the thin beams.

To eat in someone else's garden is a luxury beyond measure. The hum of friendly chatter, the raucous laughter, confidences shared in low tones. There is also the opportunity to drink up the delights of another gardener's work. There are pots of deep-claret and rust dahlias, pink cosmos in Victorian terracotta pots and pelargoniums grown straggly with age. Madonna lilies grow tall through branching stands of fennel and swaying sprays of *Verbena bonariensis*. Shorter plants are almost lost in a sea-froth of *Ammi majus*.

I am jealous of my hosts' potted hostas. The ridged green leaves are catnip for slugs and snails and none has lasted so much as a day in my garden. The sun is almost painful today (it is the hottest day of the year) and we sit in the shade of the vine drinking home-made lemonade. There is, thankfully, no hot food – who could bear to put the oven on in this heat? – so we eat salads of mozzarella and allot-ment-grown tomatoes; a platter of new potatoes, peas and Parma ham and another of lettuces and French beans. There are ice creams for dessert, one made with home-grown plums and another with raspberry ripple.

There is something fragrant to touch at every turn; scented geranium leaves to rub or pots of thyme to tear at. Such temptations would be spotted at any time of year but today, in this scorching sunshine, everything is heightened; the intensity of rose oil from the pelargonium leaves, lemon from the thyme and even the peppermint and pepper and notes of potted basil sing loud and true in the bright sunlight. Butterflies – pale-blue hoppers, cabbage whites and even red admirals – head from bloom to bloom, one even coming to see what is on my plate.

At the Taj Mahal, just after dawn, the sky is lavender, grey and orange. I notice that the walls of the vast marble mausoleum are not white but a soft and time-aged ivory, and much more beautiful than I had ever dreamed.

The habit of eating

A drought. The first for thirty years. The soil around the rose bushes is pale and cracked, like the rind of old Cheddar. You would need a chisel to work the ground. Some of the topiary yew domes in their terracotta pots have given up the ghost, their needles straw-coloured and tinder-dry.

I am writing my Sunday column in the shade of the medlar tree, the air heavy and still, the words coming slowly. Even the bees have given up their trips in search of nectar. The butterflies are out, no doubt cooled by pale-blue wings twice the size of their bodies. For once in this city, there is almost total silence.

It is early; few of my neighbours are stirring. I ponder the idea of breakfast: a slice of chilled melon, a bowl of skyr or a slice of yesterday's summer pudding I know is part-submerged in a puddle of crimson juice in the fridge. I could cut a slice of treacle bread or fetch a short crackle-crusted baguette from the shop to eat with ice-cold butter. There is rice to steam and eat with luminous purple and green pickles from Japan, cold peaches from Provence and thin slices of air-dried ham from Italy. I could make a bowl of porridge.

For the first time in years, I realise that I neither want nor need anything. I assume I am hungry because I am in the habit of eating at this time each day, not because I am really in need of sustenance. Instead I want for nothing, enjoying the soft ache of an empty stomach. It is an extraordinary feeling, but one I am happy with and rather wish I would notice more often.

The comfort of rice

Steaming rice, roasted green tea. It is the scent of home, of safety. To smell steaming rice in the early morning is as comforting as being a baby swaddled in a cashmere shawl.

In a cheap business hotel your grains will come from an ugly plastic rice cooker; in a country ryokan, where you will breakfast in a padded gown and slippers, they will more likely be kept warm in a cast-iron rice pot with a wooden lid. The smell of warm rice and wood. You take the flat wooden spoon at its side and scoop your sticky, glutinous rice into a bowl; you shuffle along the counter to the dishes of accompaniments. There will be jewel-bright tsukemono in tiny bowls, crisp pickles of deep-green cucumber and yellow radish, turnips and mustard greens.

A bowl of rice. Not too much, gently mounded, sticky or with each long grain separate from the others. Silent, white, pure. Sitting quietly in its bowl, devoid of adornment, it is quite the most beautiful thing on earth. A little bowl of calm.

A bowl of rice is a blank canvas on which we can paint. I season it as the mood takes me. There are no rules, unless you are someone unable to shed the shackles of tradition, but I do feel some seasonings are more comfortable than others, depending on the texture of the rice. At home, a bowl of long-grain white rice will get a stream of melted butter and a crumbling of sea salt and then, as I turn the grains slowly in the warm, golden fat, perhaps a grating of Parmesan, then a little black pepper and lemon juice. A bowl of sticky rice feels more at home with sansho pepper or toasted sesame seeds, crumbs of dried nori and some crisp pickled radish.

Another day I will heat the meat juices left over from the Sunday roast and stir them into the rice, streaking them with ribbons of glistening mahogany.

In the food hall of a department store in Osaka, flat plastic packets of rose-pink cherry blossom on twigs. Just as we would sell herbs.

A cocktail by the fire
Lapland

In Lapland, snow falling, curled up on the sofa by a blazing fire, I am offered the cocktail menu.

Espresso-flavoured vodka, sweetgrass and mushroom
Vodka, birch and lemon
Lingonberry vodka, baby spruce and rose
Islay single malt and cloudberry
Lingonberry, spruce and elderflower

I'm not much of a cocktail drinker, but I do love a menu with a sense of place, so I sit and sip notes of fresh green spruce and garnet-red berries in the light of the fire, the colours glowing like sunlight through a stained-glass window.

Packing a suitcase

A suitcase is never empty. Each one is so full of plans, hopes and dreams that there is barely room for clothes. No wonder we have to sit on it to get it to shut.

My original suitcase was a dog-eared Globetrotter that travelled with me to Florence and Santiago, New York and Bangkok, Accra, Athens and Delhi. It retired with a broken lock and so many stickers it was refused permission to board by a grump at the check-in counter in Bogotá. He scraped off each proud stamp with a wallpaper stripper he kept in his pocket and quietly broke a traveller's heart.

My current case was a present from James for my sixtieth birthday. Its fat, stitched-leather handles whisper, 'I am a traveller.' Each ridged aluminium side wears its dents and scratches, scuffs and scrapes as proudly as a member of a fight club flaunts his bruises. The four chrome corners already show the scars of unseen battles with baggage handlers and airport carousels. The tattoos of travel. It is the best present I have ever been given.

Packing a suitcase shows my OCD for the gift that it is. A neatly filled case, its contents held safe by tight elastic straps, is a thing of joy. A celebration of folding, stacking and rolling. A Jenga-like arrangement of T-shirts and socks, tracksuits and trainers. A completed jigsaw of carefully edited outfits suited to the season and destination, each gathered and placed into one of six black zip-fastened travel bags.

I have honed my cargo over many years. It is a ruthlessly edited capsule wardrobe for the traveller. There are time-worn, ring-spun cotton T-shirts made on machines invented in the 1830s; old-fashioned thermal long-johns with button flies and a pair of soft woollen slippers. There are socks of only one colour, a tracksuit so smart you can wear it for breakfast or for a drink at the smartest hotel bar and a single blue linen handkerchief folded up like a piece of origami. There is a simple roll-neck woollen jumper for cold days and a stiff leather box of chargers and adapters with a brass zip. A light, quilted pilot's jacket with a hood deals with the worst the winter can muster and refuses to crease even when needed to double as a pillow.

My packing is practised and artful. If an item is not deemed essential, it is left behind. I don't do 'just in case'. Nothing comes along for the ride. Not one extra sock. Underwear? A pair to wear, a pair for spare and one for the wash. In my book the hotel laundry is the best invention since the airplane. There is quiet relief in returning to your room after a day's walking to find a basket of freshly washed and ironed clothes. Especially for someone who does his own for the rest of the year. Most hotels have long dispensed with the wasteful plastic bags and wire hangers. In a Japanese ryokan you may find that your much-loved frayed T-shirts come back lovingly folded and wrapped in tissue in a linen box and tied with a voluminous cotton furoshiki.

I suppose I should tell you about the lists. Friends laugh (oh, how they laugh), but my notes of what to pack, carefully red-pencilled over the years (if something wasn't used, it is never invited again), enable me to pack swiftly and with a certain economy of space. There are lists for long haul and short haul, for summer and winter, and for my check-in and carry-on. The lists are both on my phone and in fountain pen in my notebook. I edit each one whilst I am travelling, removing anything unused and adding something I wish I had packed. A small pair of travel scissors, for instance.

There is more. There is a list for each of the six black zip-up laundry bags; every pocket of my canvas carry-on and what I wear to travel. I know which zip to pull in order to find my sunglasses and which pouch carries the old brown leather purse in which I store my travel receipts. People can mock, but I am the guy who can pack for a long-haul journey, with nothing taken unnecessarily and nothing forgotten, in a matter of minutes. Then my case is still full of plans, hopes and dreams, but I don't have to sit on it to close it.

I know Helsinki Airport better than any other. Arriving in Finland one winter's afternoon, I am greeted by a massive sign in airport arrivals bearing the slogan: 'Nobody in their right mind would come to Helsinki in November. Except you, you badass. Welcome.'

A welcome dinner in Iran
Tehran

We stop at a petrol station on the road to Tehran. Not only do they have packets of the original custard creams, but orange and banana flavour too. The existence of banana-flavoured custard creams is something I am rather pleased to know about.

The first thing I eat in Iran is white cheese, dry and crumbly, on white plates decorated with pink roses. A sheet of flatbread folded like a book. There are coarsely ground walnuts and a glass bowl of pomegranate molasses, sticky as treacle.

The cheese is followed by a dish of white rice with a dark-green – almost black – slurry of herbs and pink beans, round flatbreads and a red plastic bowl of mint leaves, green and purple basil and chives. We sit cross-legged on the floor round a plastic tablecloth decorated with pink tulips. This is the first of many versions of khoresh-e ghormeh sabzi, the herb and bean stew that will sustain us throughout the entire trip. This one is without the usual lamb and is thick with chopped fenugreek.

Sitting at a wooden counter in the market, I am asked by my director to drink tea from a heavy glass cup whilst looking thoughtful. There is one of these shots in almost every television travel programme. The tea is brown, like malt vinegar. I pretend to think about the human rights issues in the country we are in when in truth all I am thinking about is that the cup isn't particularly clean. Later we return to the counter to eat a soup of potatoes and chickpeas, bright with turmeric. It tastes a bit earthy and almost drab until the elderly man leans over the counter with a plate of halved limes to squeeze over and dinner spectacularly comes to life.

Night bathing
Japan and Korea

That's when you see them ... the ghosts.

As the steam rises from the water, soft, slowly moving clouds that waft in the night air, you see them. I watch them swirling amongst the rocks that line the edges of the outdoor bath and the trees whose leaves offer a discreet glimpse of the bathers to those walking along the paths, their steps lit only by occasional glowing tōrō, the low stone lanterns that illuminate the garden. The steam vanishes and you are left with the night sky and its stars. The only sound is the occasional clink-clonk of wooden geta on the path and the whispering swish of a passing yukata.

Bathing alone, outdoors and at night, is when you see the ghosts. Perhaps they are the spirits of those who have also sat here naked under the stars, calmed by the silence of the night and the warmth of the water. Those, too, who have watched the mist swirling in the night sky, like milk slowly poured into amber tea.

Winter nights are best, when your body is warm under the water and the frost prickles your face. When you must watch your step on the newly frosted path to the wooden changing room, the grey stones having been worn smooth by centuries of wet feet.

There are noises, muffled and mysterious. The sound of the water breathing. Soft rustling from the spindly magnolia and azalea bushes that surround the onsen. A leaf falling from its twig, a mouse or vole on an adventure perhaps, or, heaven forbid, a rat.

Could it be a snuffling hedgehog? A squirrel would surely make more noise. Whatever, its presence feels harmless here.

I remain still, moving my hands occasionally to send ripples through the cosseting water. It is so quiet I can hear the movement of the noren – the split curtain that hangs in place of a door – and footsteps on the tatami matting. I hear slippers being placed on a wooden shelf, yukata and the shorter, thicker hanten jacket being folded and placed in one of the rows of wicker baskets that stand in for lockers, and know I am to be joined. As my fellow bather gives a nod of acknowledgement and steps silently into the water, I remind myself that they are a kindred spirit rather than an invader.

Night bathing feels different to that done in the early morning. More meditative, a time to reflect rather than refresh. Enveloped in warm, still water, with just the scent of witch hazel or winter jasmine carried by the steam, the body, if not the spirit, feels at prayer.

One night I will fall asleep in the onsen, my head slowly sinking under the water, never to return. I cannot tell you how happy I would be to leave that way.

Down in the village, wandering the stone paths that lead down to the public onsen, I come across a shop, so small you enter just two at a time, selling cream puffs like clouds, full of soft, sweet custard and dusted with icing sugar.

Burning incense

The single line of smoke is caught in a draught from the morning-room window. Wandering slightly, as if someone unseen is blowing it gently off course. The smoke twists to the left, shudders and dips, then corrects itself and continues in a straight line towards the ceiling. The room smells of smoke, old books and cedar and something I can't quite put my finger on. A note that moves back and forth, something ancient, possibly tar-based. (It is actually bois de cade – juniper wood – of which I keep a small glass vial on my desk.)

I am a latecomer to incense, having smelled too much cheap stuff in my twenties, most of it used as nothing more than a distraction, an overpowering, often hideously sweet scent to disguise everything from the smell of damp to weed. As with so many things, there is incense and there is incense.

I have risen at dawn to avoid the queues. I come to see the temple that rests like a becalmed galleon amongst the acers and immaculately raked gravel but end up being more interested in its smell than its long history or function. I stand in awe not of the building's craftsmanship and ancient timbers but of the smell of the place. (It is always the smell. The older I get, the more I measure something with my nose, be it a book, a city or an item of clothing.) The incense that burns in this sacred place has permeated every plank of honed and well-worn wood right up to the rafters. It is hundreds of years of burning incense that holds this place together as much as any wooden nail.

I never track down the actual essence, but I do find out its maker, who has been making incense since the seventeenth century. I tie myself in knots trying their wares.

Incense is an accessary to worship, an offering to the gods, but I use it simply to make an unknown space my own. I pack a few sticks and a holder as small and thin as a coin in my luggage. I find a faint hint, a wisp, of a familiar smell curiously grounding. I know where I am. I feel safe. It settles my spirit.

The waiting staff are pouring tea as fast as I can drink. Pale tea the colour of straw that smells of jasmine. With steaming baskets of dim sum on the table too, I wonder if this is possibly the best smell on earth.

Light snow, dove-grey sky, even indoors the cold air prickles my face. The mountains are dark shadows, just visible through the mist. I sit, looking out at the falling snow, listening to the wind chimes outside. A single tinkling bell.

The sound of shuffling slippers behind me, and a kindly lady has brought me tea. Pale-green sencha in a glass cup. The tea is warm, just, mild and grassy. Rather than cradle it as I normally would, I hold the glass cup up to the snowy light, watching the snowflakes fall.

A pilgrimage of sorts
Mashhad, Iran

Outside the station, under a pink early-morning sky, we get our first taste of the city second only to Mecca on the pilgrim route. The smiles that have brightened our journey so far evaporate. The gaze from our taxi driver is that of suspicion, not welcome. We load our luggage into the back of his battered minibus and clamber into hot seats spilling their stuffing. We open the windows, then close them again as the cabin fills with the smell of leaking diesel.

Like every 'twenty-minute' drive here it takes an hour to get to our hotel. We are getting used to the free-for-all, horn-honking chaos of Iran's roads. My hotel room is the length of a football pitch, golden nets hanging at the windows, filling the space with soft silver light. The sofa and chairs are Barbara Cartland-pink. The floor is honey-toned marble. It is like Esher in the 1960s. There is a connecting door to the next room. Locked.

Mashhad is a place of pilgrimage and like all such places heaves with commerce. By which I probably mean trinkets. We are hassled at every turn to buy a carpet, a packet of saffron or a smoothie. Within minutes I am accosted by the local equivalent of the lucky heather seller, then subjected to the bump-and-grab technique of attempted pickpocketing so popular in crowded places. They fail. Eyes watch the crew's every move, checking out the contents of our vans rammed with camera equipment.

Teenagers in fake designer clothes mill around in groups. They ask us where we are from, breaking into smiles and words of welcome when we tell them. The feeling we need to watch our bags, our wallets, our backs takes us by surprise. An insecurity we have not come across on this trip. On a noisy thoroughfare I struggle to do several pieces to camera about my first impressions of the city, biting my tongue about the commercial exploitation of religious pilgrims the world over. Lucky heather anyone?

We walk towards the mosque, sure that our filming permissions are all in place. It has taken months, two years actually, to get permission to film inside the mosque. The first disappointment of our trip comes as we learn that, despite the paperwork to say otherwise, we will not be allowed to film after all. Even an accidental trespass six feet over the limit results in our fixers being taken away and questioned. Until now we have met nothing but kindness, hospitality and welcome. But here, in the holy city, I feel uneasy.

The cameras safely back in the van, James and I head for the mosque and its sacred golden shrine. The welcome as we hand over our shoes is heart-warming. We are given sour cherry sweets and smiles. Nobody stops us taking pictures other than ourselves. I feel uncomfortable with photographing people at prayer even if everyone else snaps the assembled worshippers, kneeling on the vast array of Persian carpets covering the outer courtyard. Some are indeed at worship, but many others are just resting away from the city's clogged streets, taking selfies or holding hands. I have always wanted to live in a climate where you can take the carpets outside.

A seated man bows right down, his head touching the floor in prayer, then sits up to answer his mobile as it suddenly rings. I wonder if his prayer has been answered.

Inside, the mosque is cool and crowded. Much is shrouded in scaffolding and sheets. We decide that is why the cameras have been suddenly denied access. The ceilings dazzle us. Mirrored room follows mirrored room, shimmering under the chandeliers. Bling for the pilgrims.

The architecture and geometry are mesmerising. The mirrored ceilings dripping with lights are trippy. It is like tiptoeing through a Fabergé egg. I find myself distressed rather than impressed by such extravagance amidst such appalling poverty.

We move through the exquisitely tiled rooms slowly, respectfully. We reach the shrine, pushed and jostled by a crowd desperate to touch the ornate relic itself, holding their children on their shoulders so they, too, may touch. Guards with feather dusters move dawdlers quietly on. Worshippers traditionally walk backwards away from the shrine. I would, but it is too crowded for me to do so without treading on toes, although I do my best.

The awe is palpable. The mosque is shimmering, as magnificent and splendid as any building could ever be. It is not my world and I find the glitz overpowering, a bit naff, but I am chastened by being made to feel so welcome.

As we put our shoes back on we follow the steady, rhythmic beating of drums that has been in the background like a slow heartbeat.

We leave the square and its vast expanse of Persian carpets. It is only now, in a dusty yard outside, that I am suddenly overcome, almost tearful. A procession of worshippers, dressed in black jeans and shirts, move step by slow step to the banging of an earth-shaking drum, flagellating themselves to the beat in a way I associate more with the Opus Dei. There is a touch of *Eyes Wide Shut* about the scene. Haunting, humbling, curiously shocking. I leave shaking with emotion but I am not quite sure why.

The food in Mashhad is exactly what you might expect in a tourist trap. So much so that we make a bolthole of the hotel coffee shop, retiring from the bustle and disappointment, drinking coffee milkshakes and eating tiramisu on 1960s black-leather armchairs.

* * *

The local market is a labyrinth of spice traders and knock-off train-ers. We visit the only man who doesn't pester us to see his wares and stock up on saffron, cardamom and sugar crystal sticks as gifts. The saffron is weighed out like the gold it is, sealed into tiny packets and slipped into an envelope like a Class-A drug. The jade-green cardamoms are the best I have ever encountered, more intense and resinous even than those I have bought in Kerala. I buy three pack-ets, knowing that at least one will be opened in tomorrow's cooking scene and the rest will spill in my luggage.

Looking for some tomatoes good enough to appear on camera (epic fail, presenter tantrum), my mood is lifted by the discovery of a generously stocked grain shop. The sight of snow-white sacks of barley and wheat, dried beans of exemplary quality, whole, cracked and shelled walnuts, dried roses and several varieties of rice makes us feel better and appreciate that we are surrounded by desert, so any vegetable is likely to be a little exhausted by the time it gets here.

I have decided to make a carrot salad with a dressing using the local saffron. The colours will be jewel-like, an homage to the shimmer-ing mosque. My carrot salad idea comes to grief when I find that the long, thin carrots I had assumed did rather well in the area's fine sand are actually bussed in from the other side of the country. Instead, I decide to make a soup based on the lentil ones that appear at breakfast but using tiny turnips and herbs, the only two decent fresh ingredients I could lay my hands on. I suspect the herbs are grown in people's gardens. The turnips are less damaged by the journey.

We have left our shopping to the last minute and plan to do most of it first thing in the morning en route to the location, a set of ruins in the desert. Every shop is closed, so in desperation, and using our best sign language, we beg the security guards to open up the city's largest supermarket for us.

I have never been in a vast, closed supermarket before. Alone except for a handful of bewildered shelf-fillers, there is much skating around on shopping trolleys and we eventually manage to locate double cream and herbs and stock up on water and sweeties for the crew. What surprises me is the ease with which I can buy frozen chicken Kiev or twenty types of chocolate biscuit yet not so much as a single decent vegetable.

We drive for two hours, the last few miles across dusty desert roads. The ruins make a dramatic location to cook in, with the guards showing us around the restorations and taking photographs with us all. It is all a bit Indiana Jones, setting up my camping stove in a sheltered spot between two crumbling walls.

The scene goes rather well, despite a brisk breeze continually blowing out the gas stove and the threat of missing our next plane hanging over us. You can't tell from the film, but one sudden step backwards and I could fall to my death down a virtually bottomless dry well just two feet behind me.

In Helsinki I stop at a tiny café. My camomile tea, the colour of absinthe, comes in an individual glass pot placed on its own tiny golden cushion, like a crown.

An encounter with a troll
Bergen, Norway

Bergen is crisp and snowy. I climb the stairs in Julehuset, the Christmas shop on Holmedalsgården, and explore the several rooms dedicated to baubles and tinsel, Christmas lights, snow globes and reindeer.

At the top of the stairs is a tiny room with wooden walls. On the floor, table and shelves are fifty or so elves and goblins in their winter coats and red hats. None is cute (some are downright ugly, the stuff of nightmares); these were trolls from the mountains, sinister little guys you wouldn't want at the bottom of your garden. I forget how well Scandinavia does the darker side of Christmas.

These are the pixies, elves and hobgoblins of the forest, the ones who revel in evil doings, who will cause mischief to anyone who crosses their path. I wonder, briefly, what such creatures eat for their dinner. Whatever it is, it will be eaten from a wooden bowl with a wooden spoon.

Particularly sinister is a woman with a red jumper, wooden clogs and grey plaits. She has searching blue eyes that seem to look deep into my soul. I am perplexed why anyone would want any of these in their home, unless it is to ward off intruders or evil spirits. It would be a brave burglar who crosses her path.

I am not easily spooked. As a child I loved the darker fairy tales, the stories of the Brothers Grimm and anything that involved woods and forests. I am rarely happier than in the company of M. R. James or Edgar Allan Poe. And yet I feel a certain wonder, accompanied by a shudder down the spine, as if moths were trapped in my clothes.

There are fresh barberries in the market in Tehran. Wicker hampers of oval pink berries on the twig, still with their leaves attached. The fruits have a lemony punch and I long to buy some to thread through warm couscous, as I would the dried ones.

Mulberries and a waterfall
Croatia

The air is hot enough to bake bread, the only sound is the chirruping of crickets. The ground is cracked and dry and I walk through fields of wildflowers whose crisp stems prickle my feet and scratch my bare, reddening legs. My water bottle is almost empty, my sandals are collecting tiny, obstinate thistles. I trudge in the direction of a cluster of trees in the hope of shade.

There is a drystone wall I must first negotiate, scratching my already stinging arms and legs on the rough stones. The stones are splattered with deep ruby-red and I rest under the shade of a gnarled tree whose leaves are the size of side plates. Hanging under each is a cluster of soft, ripe mulberries, glistening like garnets.

I must have sat there for twenty minutes, gorging myself on the most heavenly fruit I had ever eaten. My lips, beard and fingers were soaked in juice, my T-shirt splattered like that of a serial killer on a spree. Red rivulets are running down my arms like veins and my skin is sticky enough to attract wasps.

I plough on, legs and arms prickled with heat, thirsty despite my feast, tired enough to drop. As I reach the trees the ground seems to drop away and I can hear the roar of water. I scramble down the narrow sandy path to a deep, blue-green pool below. With no one else there, I strip and clamber in. I have no idea how long I stand, motionless, under the crashing waterfall, letting the cold, bright water wash away the dust and mulberry juice from my stinging, now heavily sunburnt skin.

It infuriates me that the entire month I spent in Italy in my late twenties was with a friend whose principal interest in travel was how many miles we could drive each day, and who delighted in marking the heroically long journeys in felt-tip pen on a map before bed. I could have learned more about Italian art, food and life by watching an episode of *Inspector Montalbano*.

Yuzu and a winter welcome
Kyushu, Japan

A long drive through the Japanese countryside and we pull up outside a wooden inn. I pay the driver and step into the deserted hallway, missing the usual restrained greeting, the welcoming half-bow. I am left alone to wander, to try to find the person who will take me to my room. I try a weak 'hello', to which there is no reply.

What welcomes me instead in this hall with its artfully burnt black wooden walls is an old tansu chest with ornate iron hinges, and on it an earthenware bowl of yuzu, the fruit glowing against the black wall. Whilst I wait for some sort of acknowledgment, I pick up a single fruit, squeeze, and then pierce the knobbly yellow skin with my thumbnail. A spritz of juice as fine as perfume from an atomiser fills the cool winter air in the hallway. Citrus, most definitely, but also spicy, a little peppery perhaps.

I tend to travel in Japan in winter and early spring. Citrus season. Against a background of leafless trees and grey sky heavy with snow, the fruits – orange, yellow, citrine flushed with green – come at you with their piercing juice. The small, sour green sudachi that is often used to flavour ponzu sauce; the kumquat-like kinkan and the seriously sour green kabosu. There are sweet oranges too, the larger gourd-like dekopon – a sweet hybrid that is often presented as a single fruit on a small, dark dish, the flesh scooped from its shell and filled with a jelly made from its juice.

Many Japanese citrus are prized for their zest as much as they are for their flesh. The yuzu and iyokan – the second-most grown variety – are candied for decorating little sponge cakes or dried, ground to a powder and added to sesame seeds and spices for seasoning rice.

You can also make tea with the dried peel, a drink to warm your heart on a frosty afternoon. Like today, when a receptionist finally shuffles towards me, gently bowing and bearing a glass cup of yuzu tea on a silver tray. A fragrant, spirit-lifting welcome to a tired traveller. She leaves me to drink my glowing tea in peace and the snow starts to fall.

In the market in Rasht, northern Iran, a linen sack the size of an oil drum filled to the brim with dried rose petals the colour of a wine stain.

A train journey through the snow
Norway

A window seat on a green train. We chug through conifer forests and along the shore with low wooden houses painted in shades of ochre with black doors. We pass ravines and waterfalls and tiny stations whose platforms are white with snow. We pass through frost-covered woods, like black-and-white lino prints in a book of fairy tales. I listen to the playlist I put together for such journeys, all the time eating tiny red apples from a paper bag and drinking cups of hot chocolate.

We travel so close to the trees you can see the frozen necklaces of spiders' webs, hoof prints in the snow, the low sun glowing here and there through the shadows like a lantern.

Past the mountains the light falls, homes are lit, the weather changes. I arrive in Bergen to wind and driving sleet. My umbrella is useless, the journey to my hotel too short to take a cab, so I walk and arrive bedraggled and drink red wine by the fire.

That moment, on holiday, when you realise that no one you can hear or see is British. No one around you speaks English. You know, for once, you have picked the right place.

A greeting of shoes

The steps are littered with abandoned shoes. Worn-out trainers and knackered leather boots, a pair of sandals with a broken strap, flip-flops so thin they barely exist are dropped where they are taken off, not even arranged in pairs. There are women's shoes as wide as they are long and children's sandals, scuffed and dusty. Iran, like so much of the Middle East, is cruel to shoes. All are down at heel, on their last legs so to speak. A carelessly strewn huddle for me to navigate.

Shoes greet your arrival in Japan too, though these will be set in a neat and soldierly line, toes facing outwards, clearly well cared for. Most will be whisked away by unseen hands, hidden from sight and only brought out as you leave. In most cases they will be exchanged for slippers, sometimes comfortable and easy, at other times wooden-soled and too small for my feet.

In the pod hotels you can tell the nationality of each cubicle's occupant by the way in which the slippers are placed outside. Left and right close together, toes facing the door, will most likely signify a local sleeping within. Left higgledy-piggledy, the resident is more likely to be a traveller, a tourist.

The habit of removing your shoes on entering a building is annoying to someone who wears lace-up boots as I often do. I have learned to travel in slip-ons, particularly in Japan and the Middle East, where life involves a change of footwear to enter a museum, a hotel or even some shops. At the Raku Museum in Kyoto, a peaceful and thoughtfully curated collection of tea bowls and the very devil to find, you are asked to swap your shoes for covetable jade-green velvet slippers. You may find yourself not wishing to give them back.

It is a habit I would be happy to adopt if my own floors were less full of gashes, lumps and splinters. We have no such formality, except for those entering the drawing room, which has always been a shoes-off room. A room where, incidentally, no laptops are allowed either.

Feeding the birds
Helsinki, Finland

The wind nips my ears; my cheeks prickle. Earlier in the morning there had been a light fall of snow in Helsinki and I arm myself with woolly hat and gloves, scarf and hoodie. Passengers, many drunk, tumble from the blue boats that have just arrived from Estonia. On the harbour there are tarpaulin tents and the smell of fish frying on metal trays the size of cartwheels. Each tray comes with potatoes and rosemary. I stand in line with my paper plate.

The tables in the tent are taken by families and excited children sharing their lunch over the chequered plastic cloths. I move outside, my plate bending under the weight of my lunch. At which moment a gull the size of a small plane crashes onto the plate of the woman next to me. There is much flapping and squawking, mostly from the woman, who is struggling not to lose her lunch. Amidst the clicking of phone cameras, the bird rises into the sky, up and up, fillet of fish proudly in his beak.

Waking to snow

Snow has fallen overnight. The blackbird is silent. No rumble of traffic. Only the occasional pfuff as a tiny avalanche of snow falls from the leaves of the heavily laden beech tree.

The dark-green needles of the yew hedges peep through here and there and bird tracks pepper the path. There are the clear, deep paw prints of the fox. Other than that the world seems asleep, as if it has opened one eye, seen the thick white blanket that has settled overnight, then pulled the duvet up round its chin and gone back to sleep.

I put the kettle on. Green tea, a clementine with its leaf and a dish of yoghurt no bigger than a shot glass. I light a candle and settle down at the kitchen table to write. The peace of early morning I so love is going on for longer today. Just the hum of the fridge and the occasional crunch of footsteps on the stone flags outside as someone trudges bravely to work.

Snow falls so rarely in London. It is only now, the unsightly hidden under a blanket of white, that you remember how beautiful parts of the city are, how handsome some of its architecture and how majestic its plane trees. The snow briefly masks the city's flaws, its litter and concreted-over front gardens. It muffles the constant noise.

I cherish this moment. Just the shuffle of snow as it starts its inevitable thaw; the smell of clementine and woodsmoke; the sound of my pen nib scratching on paper.

The sweet shop
Pateley Bridge, North Yorkshire

I am filming a documentary about sweets, and we arrive at the dearly loved World's Oldest Sweetshop, where fans queue for a pink-and-white striped bag of nostalgia.

Even before we enter the shop with its tinkling bell to meet the kindly owner, I stand mesmerised at the window with its merry-go-round and glass jars of dragées and marshmallows. My eyes widening as I spot a fat tin of Riley's chocolate toffee rolls and another of Brown Brothers' rhubarb and custards, Doncaster toffee and another still of Parkinson's butterscotch. Here is the home of Wilkinson's Pontefract cakes and orange, black and white jelly babies. There are fizz balls and jelly buttons, Winter Mixture, and foil-wrapped butterscotch, pips, bullets and sherbons. It is here in Nidderdale that fat glass jars hold Finnish Liquorice and Dutch Crowns, where mint humbugs are safe and where eau de Nil and rose bon bons shall be stocked for ever. Where the owner stands guardian, protecting the future of Nuttall's Mintoes and sugared almonds, Marry-me Quicks and Judy Barretts, Rainbow Kali and Coltsfoot Rock.

Sugar in every shape and shade. The crew usher me in and we film this living museum of candy. I leave, suddenly seven years old again, clutching bags of treacle dabs and chocolate-coated toffees. My childhood spelled out in sugar.

Snow falling on the mountain path. A long line of Japanese people, all dressed in black with vivid-orange umbrellas.

Maritozzi
Florence

I notice how often my day starts with white food. Pure, simple, unsullied, like a new page in a diary. A Goldilocks's bowl of porridge in Scotland. A thin glass dish of yoghurt in Beirut. Steamed rice in Taiwan and a plate of sheep's cheeses in Iran with a flick of green mint and pink pickled radish.

Here, on this nippy autumn morning, I breakfast on bitter coffee in a cup the size of a thimble and a single white maritozzo, a small dome of sweet brioche, round and plump, split across the top and filled with whipped and lightly sweetened cream. There are specks of vanilla in the cream as fine as dust and the crown of the bun is smooth and freckled with a soft fall of white icing sugar.

This was not meant to be. The idea of a cream bun for breakfast makes me feel slightly queasy, but I am travelling so I will go with the flow.

From the icing sugar on the tip of my nose to the dot of whipped cream caught on my top lip, everything about this bun is a surprise. The dough is pillow-soft, the cream as white as a nun's wimple and very cold, as if a little iced water has been whipped in (and I expect it has). The dough, the cream, the extreme lightness of it all takes me by surprise. Not sickly or cloying as you might expect. It is, of course, another white breakfast. Pure, simple, unsullied.

Lighting the fire
Norway

Flåm, Norway, the rain pricking our skin like needles. We arrive at our accommodation, a white-walled cottage as cold as the grave. It smells of smoke, fir and fish. We hang our wet anoraks over the backs of chairs, light chubby beeswax candles, put the kettle on the stove, then set about lighting the fire. There are dry twigs and kindling in the fireplace that flare up, cracking and popping the second they are lit. In minutes we are as warm as buttered toast.

It has been too long since I made a fire out of necessity. Growing up, an open fire was the only heating we had, the logs and coals being piled up before bed so the embers would still be glowing in the morning. Even with a fireguard round the hearth we were lucky the house didn't burn down as we slept.

From the moment you strike the match, a fire is a thing of geniality and beauty – the fingers of rough-edged kindling, the bundles of crisp, dry twigs resting on fat logs. The sparks as you strike the long match on the matchbox and the way the first skinny twigs catch alight. There is a crackle and the occasional pop, a streak of flame and then a single line of smoke. Flames on which to warm your hands, smoke to make your jumper smell like home.

The warmth is only part of the blessing of a fire. Each flicker brings with it a brief moment of magic. A dance. A daydream. To gaze into the flames of an open fire is to go down a rabbit hole. This fire brings with it flickering images of tintype photographs and horse-drawn carriages, but you can choose your rabbit hole. All you need do is stare; the flames will take you wherever you wish to go.

Once lit, you long to stay at its side with a book – a ghost story surely – and perhaps something in a glass. But not all fires are equal. The most successful woods for burning are dry ones (wet wood produces more smoke than heat) and hardwood is the best of all. It gives good flames. Oak, elm, ash and beech are the best contenders. I have used cherry, medlar and apple too, branches acquired during pruning. Wood that I kept for several months to let it dry out. This 'seasoning' produces a longer burn and less smoke.

Woods such as cherry burn particularly fragrantly, holly has a light and brilliant flame. Pine, especially old Christmas trees, produces flammable resin that can easily get out of control. Recycling is a safer option.

The room warms, the smoke plumes, we stay silent and pull the sleeves of our jumpers down over our fingers. There is coffee in the pot and, right now, this is enough.

The best sleep

The room, at the end of a long wooden corridor, is filled with early-evening winter light, softened further by the washi paper blinds. I swap my shoes for the room slippers provided and step onto the springy tatami. There is a long lacquered table with two flat cushions on either side, a wooden rail on which to hang my clothes with old wooden coat hangers, polished by the jackets of previous occupants. A tall vase with a single branch of blossom, its buds still tightly closed. An embroidered scroll hangs on the wall.

It is some time before it dawns on me that there is no bed. I open cupboards and slide back the blinds that cover the windows, I tap the walls for hidden panels or a sliding door. Mystified, I change and wander down to dinner, which turns out to be endless, a trial for a weary traveller aching for his bed.

The journey has been an ordeal. I changed trains more than once, lugged my suitcase down endless flights of steps and, having fumbled my timing, got overly familiar with one particular waiting room. The day's food has been the emergency almonds and chocolate I had squirrelled away in the pocket of my rucksack. Ten minutes before I arrived at the ryokan door it had started to rain.

As dinner ends, tea – clear, light, fragrant – is brought in a tall porcelain cup and I take it to my room, an act that seems to cause a moment of consternation amongst the staff. My room has been entered whilst I ate. A low, glowing lantern has appeared on the floor, illuminating a thick mattress tightly wrapped in crisp white cotton sheets. A quilted duvet with a purple-and-white cover of flying cranes is draped softly over the top. I peel back the sheets and slip down between them, snuggle under the cloud-like duvet and, in the soft glow of the night light, with the gentle patter of rain on the windows sleep like never before.

The pomegranate harvest
Iran

We attend the local pomegranate festival, where we are greeted by a rickety metal stand, hanging from it a newly slaughtered goat, its innards proudly displayed on a hook complete with lungs, heart and liver. Later it would be roasted over an open fire and sold.

Vast cloths lie under the trees, piles of fruit, cherubic, flashed with carmine, their flowers dried into a crown. Here and there children break open the fruits, pulling at the scarlet seeds in clusters, spitting out the papery pith, chucking the skins in the long grass. We arrive early to avoid the crowds, the thousands who flock to the festival each year, going home with armfuls, boxes and bulging bags of the fattest fruits I have ever seen.

There is no music this year, the area being still in mourning for its local imam who died a few weeks ago. But there is still a feeling of quiet celebration for a harvest that is the lifeblood of the area. We create more than usual interest, with children offering us pieces of fruit to eat, to which we can't say no, from politeness but also because it came direct from the tree, each mouthful being juicier and more refreshing than the pomegranates at home. The flavour is intense and the juice is evident over everyone's hands and clothes. The sensible wear something less likely to show the *Dexter*-esque splatter patterns.

In Istanbul I eat at a local esnaf lokantasi, the restaurants, often self-service, where working people take their lunch. As we leave I spot a fridge with foil containers of chilled rice pudding, stacked one upon another. Each has a browned skin on top, just as my father loved.

A local feast
Ireland

'You'd better bring a mug,' said my friend John over the phone as I packed to join him in Ireland, 'I've only got one.' A couple of days later, damp and shivering from a night in his tent, bleary-eyed from our evening in the local pub, we drink instant coffee to warm ourselves round the fire. I loathe instant coffee and always have done, but this morning the thin, hot liquid is heaven-sent.

I have come ill-prepared for camping. I haven't used my sleeping bag since I lent it to a friend to take to Greece the summer before. Last night I unzipped the quilted bag only to find its lining, once plain navy blue, now splattered with heaven knows what. 'It'll help keep you warm,' sniggers John. To make matters worse I have forgotten to pack any clean underwear and I am to be here for a week.

We slice delicious sausages bought from the local shop and fry them in a shallow, battered pan over a small gas stove. I want my bangers to be a deep, glossy brown. John wants to save gas. We compromise at pale gold, the bangers cooked just long enough not to give us food poisoning. Before we run out of Calor gas I pour a can of beans ceremoniously over them and tip them onto enamel plates. We laugh as we recall my innocent request in the village shop for some of the much-lauded local unpasteurised blue cheese, which they had never heard of, let alone stocked. We left instead with a budget-priced can of beans and a packet of custard creams. A feast on a morning after sleep had been interrupted by mysterious rustlings in the undergrowth. 'It's probably just a hedgehog,'

John had whispered, clearly trying to reassure himself as much as me.

My idea of feasting on local oysters and cheese, toasting soda bread over an open fire is quietly forgotten and for the rest of the trip we stuff ourselves with crisps and biscuits.

Kinosaki, February. An aluminium bowl of steamed white rice flecked with minuscule pink fish the size of orzo.

Nowruz and the sprouted seeds
Tehran

Nowruz, Persian New Year. I am perched, not exactly comfortably, on my friend's rather upright sofa. A vase of faded maroon silk flowers sits on the marble coffee table in front of me, around it a collection of white dishes filled with seeds, lentils, barley and wheat at differing stages of sprouting. Some are straight from the jar, newly damp, others a good twenty centimetres or so high, have been growing for a fortnight in preparation for today.

There are more white dishes of sprouts on the sideboard and another tucked amongst the leather-bound tomes on the bookshelf. A symbol of good luck for the coming year, they are to be admired rather than eaten. Having seen little in the way of green leaves on my plate for a good week or two, I just want to grasp tufts of the bright-green shoots and stuff them into my mouth.

A tuckbox on the train

I remove the blue rubber band that secures the lid. The cool smell of cucumber wafts up. (The blue rubber band has had a previous life holding together a bunch of asparagus. They are the best rubber bands and I save them in the drawer in the kitchen.) I peep inside. I know what is in my lunchbox, I have packed it myself, but its contents nevertheless feel like a surprise.

A tuckbox is always a treat, settling comfortably into the category of 'self-gifting'. This morning's package, fodder to accompany a train trip to York, consists of a rye bread sandwich filled with salmon and cucumber, a repurposed Neal's Yard yoghurt pot of cold roast vegetables and a slice of ginger cake. The latter is wrapped in a brown greaseproof paper bag that I buy in boxes from the health food store. I wish I'd had the foresight to squirrel away a Tunnock's Caramel Wafer or a tube of Rolos, if only for the seasoning of nostalgia, but I haven't.

The peat-brown bread is chosen for its ability to fill (especially the one with pumpkin seeds embedded in its tight, treacly crumb), and its neat, square edges fit precisely into the corners of the box. The lid doubles as a tray so I don't leave a Hansel and Gretel-esque trail of crumbs for the next traveller. There's no room for an apple, and I have a pathological fear of travelling with a banana due to an unmentionable incident involving a duffle bag on a school trip to Ludlow. A tumble of blueberries it is. Cake is an absolute essential. A tuckbox without cake is pretty much unthinkable to this traveller. Ideally a slice of fruit cake, but when did I last make one of those?

I have avoided bringing any of the leftover bread and butter pudding. Thinking about it now, I could have used a second yoghurt container. I could also have brought a salad, but they are almost always a bad idea. The dressing drips, the leaves unfurl or have collapsed into compost by the time you arrive at the station. A few cherry tomatoes – the children's sweeties of the vegetable box – are a fine idea and I should have thought of that.

To lift the lid on a tin or wooden box of sandwiches and treats brings untold joy to a lengthy train journey. As essential as a good book or an engaging podcast; as much fun as fumbling in the depths of a stocking on Christmas morning. In Japan I travel with a bento box bought from a kiosk on the station platform, and for some reason a bag of almonds, which I carry in the front right-hand pocket of my satchel wherever I go. In Scandinavia it will be cardamom buns in a bag. But today it is salmon and cucumber sandwiches and ginger cake.

I replace the lid on the now-empty box, retrieve the rubber band from my pocket and wriggle it into place. I am replete and feeling rather smug about my culinary forethought.

We have yet to leave the station.

Fishcakes on the lake
The Caspian Sea

This is nothing like the soft lilt and sway I was expecting. That gentle cradle-rock of being aboard a small boat on a lake.

The spray from the prow is almost blinding, my hair soaked and sticking tightly to my head. I am so cold I can barely turn my neck to see the shore and I have lost all feeling in my fingers. I pull up my hood and tighten the cord and we snake through the tall reeds, winding our way across the lake, the boat swaying violently port and then starboard, buffeted by the wind. I am somewhere between exhilaration and cardiac arrest.

The lake was once so full of sturgeon it kept the entire community in work and dinner, but it has been decimated by overfishing and pollution. The local fishermen who rely on the lake for their livelihood have been partly successful in getting the water back to a level where fish can once again breed. I arrive at the fishermen's shack in the middle of the lake, am hauled from the boat like a piece of cod and given a glass of bright tea and ten minutes to thaw out by the Calor gas fire.

The wooden-panelled room is surprisingly warm; carpeted and with loose curtains, it feels almost cosy. There is talk of clearing the rubbish floating in the water, restocking the lake with fish and rebooting the dwindling fishing industry. All four fishermen – there are no women working on the lake – look as if they have spent their lives on the open water and talk about long hours and a reduced and irregular income. They appear about seventy years old. I doubt anyone is over thirty-five.

One of the men lights a camping gas stove and we fry fillets of fish in a batter that makes even the lightest tempura feel like that from a back-street chippy on a Friday night. We tuck in. But then he shows me a recipe of his involving fish eggs that he mixes with a little egg and flour and pats into cakes; he dusts the outside with flour and fries them in a battered aluminium pan. They spit and splutter and the oil darkens, nuggets of charred crumb-crust peeling away in the heat. There are no forks so I tear the hot cake apart with my hands, which are now greasy and taste of fish. In one bite I am again eight years old, standing in short trousers at the fish-and-chip counter on Penn Road in Wolverhampton, eating fried cod's roe cakes with my father. That same salty tang, a flavour like potted fish paste and breadcrumbs. A taste of the English Midlands but in a wooden hut-on-stilts in the middle of an Iranian lake. Fodder with which to face the journey back to the shore.

Snow crabs in the market in a village in southern Japan, legs splayed, their claws tied together with rubber bands the colour of rust, sit upside down in boxes of crushed ice, twinkling like stars.

Macaroni cheese and a change of heart
New York

A bone-cold day, a book tour and I am deeply unhappy. Shredded from the flight, got lost trying to find the venue for my radio interview, had a poorly attended book signing and my chaperone doesn't seem to know whether it's Christmas or Tuesday. I have stop-offs ahead of me in Los Angeles, San Francisco, Boston, Chicago and heaven knows where else and I desperately want to go home. I have just been told that, unlike here, Boston has sold so many tickets for my talk that they have had to move the venue to the local church, so I will need to rethink the extracts I am planning to read as they are probably not the sort of thing anyone should say from a pulpit.

To make matters worse, I have just finished an interview in my hotel lounge with a journalist who clearly hated me at first sight and was from a magazine I really didn't want to be featured in anyway. That said, my hosts have been impossibly generous. Last night's restaurant dinner was so smart they had to fight the reception dragons ('fingernails as long as the heels of their stilettos') to accept my extremely smart attire as even remotely suitable. Though things got better when I found Isabella Rossellini and David Lynch at the next table. They are also putting me up in a very cool hotel where the staff are straight out of the pages of *Vogue Hommes* and I am reliably assured they will do 'anything' for you if you wave the right notes at them. In reality, the staff are all so up themselves they hand over your room key like you have leprosy and leave you to carry your own bag. Did I say I desperately wanted to go home?

Anyway, I do what I always do on such occasions and find a table in the hotel bar. For which, dear reader, I have to queue. Ravenous, I order the only thing on the menu that doesn't sound like it was invented by and for hipsters. On my second drink my mood is not better, but the glass of champagne has knocked the edge off things. And then it arrives. A vast round dish, deep as a tyre, of glistening, purring, steaming macaroni cheese.

I dip in my fork, twizzle the strands of molten cheese round its tines like spaghetti and dig back in for more of the macaroni. In one mouthful my world turns on its head; the hotel, glowing now, seems warm and friendly and the staff charming, and my frozen soul is thawing out. In one mouthful my tongue, my tummy and probably my arteries are coated with the sort of comfort only carbs and melted cheese can bring. The world is suddenly a changed place. Thank you, macaroni cheese.

In a café in Spitalfields, London. Newly made marmalade in squat glass jars sitting on the larder shelf. Pots of glowing amber, rust and cinnamon jelly, smugly waiting for toast.

The journey into Agra
India

I am unsure of how long I have been asleep, my head lolling, my body softly jolted from side to side in the back of the car. I am not sure I am awake even now.

An elephant dressed like a festival tent is walking alongside us. A sort of lumbering grace. The elephant is decorated with embroidered shawls, ribbons and marigolds and strings of bells. Men in shorts walk at its side, carefully missing its feet. On the other side of the car people walk as if on a slow, winding march, billowing clouds in candy colours, pastel mauves, soft yellows and pinks. There are jewelled turbans and long, floating shawls, laughter and, through the car's cranky air conditioning, the scent of jasmine. And all the time the constant jingling of bells, like those of a tambourine.

A holy festival, a wedding, a dream? I am not sure. I only know that I have woken, *if* I have actually woken, in the most extraordinary trance-like state, racked with tiredness and exhausted by weeks of stifling heat. I feel faintly queasy, get out of the car and walk up the steps to the hotel reception, where I am told with profuse apologies that there is no evidence of our booking to be found. Something tells me that every room in the city will be taken.

Snow in Kyushu

The further we go into the mountains, the darker green the forest. As daylight falls, with the last of the treacherous bends behind us, we get out of the bus and tramp up the path to our inn. We change our boots for soft quilted slippers. Logs crackle in the wood burner in the hall and I ache to linger, to watch the flames. Ushered along polished wooden floors, I am shown to my room. There are few other guests. The house is silent and I climb under my duvet and sleep the sleep of angels, not stirring till dawn.

No birdsong, just the early-morning light coming through the washi paper blinds, ice-white, casting a chill over the room. I get out of bed and pad down slippery wooden stairs and corridors in my thick, quilted bathrobe and slippers. Reception is deserted and the fire has burned low, so I tiptoe behind the desk to retrieve my walking boots from the neat line of guests' politely confiscated shoes. I slide open the rickety wooden door with its rattling glass panels, silence the wind chimes that announce arrival or departure, and gingerly step out onto the path.

The straggly camelias and bamboo are bowed down by the snow that has fallen during the night. The path is hidden beneath a deep white down. A thin line of grey smoke works its way from the outdoor hearth, its fat logs still burning, and there is a candle-like glow from the stone houses and hanging lanterns. Each dreamlike step crunches softly, leaving a yeti-style footprint in the snow.

After my walk, I return to find that my slippers have been placed by the wood-burning stove and a tray on which someone unseen has settled a cup of roasted hōjicha. I slide my icy toes into the warm slippers and cup the tea in my hands.

I hope, briefly, that I have passed away in my sleep and that this snowy wonderland, peace and toasted tea is what I have been praying for all these years.

Late afternoon, in December, strolling along the Kohlmarkt in Vienna. Snowflakes are falling from a grey sky, white Christmas lights twinkle above me. A gilded birdcage hangs in the window of Demel. Locked inside is a perfectly balanced pyramid of miniature marzipan apples, each with its cheeks brushed with rose-pink colouring.

A table of herbs
Tehran

We pull over and stop at the roadside. A respite from the insanity that is driving in Iran. A young man whose hands are already gnarled from hard work has set up a stall of home-grown herbs. A metal dish the size of a tractor tyre, piled with bunches of mint, dill, coriander and tarragon. Another, slightly smaller dish has bunches of white-topped radishes fresh from the soil, set round a pile of spiky rocket leaves. There are bundles of chives tied with raffia and a dish of mixed leaves like those they sell in cellophane packs in supermarkets.

The piercing scent of mint, the acute freshness of the leaves sings out against a brown and barren landscape and busy grey road, but I am perplexed: why this place, in the middle of nowhere? No pedestrians in sight and no room for more than one car to stop. He speaks no English, my Arabic is confined to greetings, pleases and thank yous. I will never know why he sets up here. But this is a regular spot: his stalks and leaves have a tin roof, a light bulb and a small and dirty generator.

I buy radishes to eat in the car, mint to quell my garlicky breath and worry about what he will do with all his herbs.

I will never cease to be charmed by the staff on the Shinkansen, smiling and bowing deeply to the carriage as they walk through to the next.

Cabin crew

I step into the cabin and feel my shoulders drop. Greetings with the crew exchanged, I find my seat, take out my book and pods, and stow my hand luggage. The dark-blue canvas bag that accompanies every flight, train or car journey. My ten-kilogram bag that holds passport, iPad, leatherbound notebook, diary, reading book and spare glasses. The bag that holds tiffin tin and tissues, wallet and woolly hat. Sitting down, I buckle up and open my book. I pull up my hood and melt into my seat.

For the next few hours someone else is in the driving seat, making the decisions. The route, the cabin temperature and what I shall have for dinner. For once, my life is in someone else's hands.

For eleven months a year I run my own life. I make every espresso and pour each glass of wine. Each decision is mine to make, and to be fair I wouldn't want it any other way. And yet, for the next few hours I will be fed and watered, and tucked up as I haven't been since I was a child. My dinner will be brought to me, a napkin unfurled and put on my table and my glass topped up. I can ask for ice cream to accompany the film; a nightcap to help me drift into sleep or an extra blanket under which to snuggle. For a few hours at least, I am as nannied as a sick child and grateful for it.

Squid on fire

Once a year, visitors come to see the firefly squid, dazzled by the minute cephalopods' luminescence in the water. The tiny females have come back to spawn. Once their work is done the year-old creatures are ready to die, and then, and only then, become of interest to the local fishermen. On the scale of sustainable seafood, they rate as high as it gets. As they are about to pop their clogs they are almost doing the ocean a favour.

This fact had escaped me for years. Faced with these spooky little sweetmeats winking at me from the depths of a celadon bowl, I had assumed I was eating outrageously young squid. A dish seasoned with the guilt that goes hand in tiny hand with gnawing at pinky-sized ribs of suckling pig, picking at live squid sashimi or sticking your fork into a melting slice of calf's liver. As anyone who has scrumped an apple or stolen the last After Eight knows, guilt is probably the most delectable seasoning of all.

They are rather more interesting than your average squid. Barely seven centimetres in length, they have virtually invisible pointy hooks on their tentacles and they emit a greeny-blue phosphorescent light which, en masse, causes the sea around them to light up. Glistening like blue Christmas lights along the beach, they are something of an April tourist attraction in Toyama Bay, Japan. It would be unforgivable not to order them in a restaurant. Even boiled, these one-year-olds can be described as toothsome. You might fancy a dipping saucer of aged soy or even some sea salt alongside. Deep-fried in frilly tempura batter, it comes as near to heaven as it is possible to get in one mouthful. And with a dab of citrus-scented yuzu kosho? Oh, yes please.

Firefly squid with rice is on the menu in Arashiyama today. The chef stirs them repeatedly, like a risotto, but more quickly, without the heavy, sleepy notes of the Italian recipe. They arrive in a heavy green stone bowl, crackle-glazed, the chips on its rim worn smooth from (literally) a hundred years of service. There are grains of soft, opalescent rice plump with dashi threaded through with roughly chopped firefly squid. No chewing. The rice and seafood simply melt. A juicy, squishy, fishy, fragrant, melting mouthful.

I pause at an olive stall in the market in Tehran. The produce is not like that in Provence, where you are offered black and purple olives too, olive oil and bars of green soap. This is just eighteen bright-pink washing-up bowls piled with green olives. They differ only slightly in size and price. Most have been cracked, stones removed. I want to taste one from each bowl but am dragged away by my crew. Frustrated.

Midnight in Mauritius

To get to the beach I must cross the cloyingly fragrant garden outside my room and negotiate the narrow path that runs through the dense foliage. I step out into the darkness, my beach towel round my neck, to the whirr-tick of crickets and the soft breeze of swooping bats.

I walk quickly, hoping the sound of pattering feet will send any snakes and lizards scuttling for cover, swishing the bushes as I walk. There is a smell, rich and sickly sweet, so pungent I feel as if I am being choked. A smell that is both new and curiously familiar. Notes of the most intense jasmine with a back note of vanilla and overripe mango.

The sea is too warm, and I cut short my night swim. As I pass through the garden, lanterns now glowing, the perfume has faded a little, it is less hypnotic, softer and more floral than before. Trumpets of deep-crimson hibiscus have closed for the night, chains of bougainvillea and a plant I do not know are the only ones in flower. It is this last from which the scent is emanating. Each blossom has thick white petals, crisp, like icing on a wedding cake. Almost too perfect to be real, the petals darken in the centre to a pale yellow with a deep-saffron eye. Strangely, the scent is stronger from a distance than close up.

My mystery flower is frangipani, or if we are talking in botanical terminology, *Plumeria*, the name given to honour the seventeenth-century French monk and botanist Charles Plumier. I note that the almond filling known as frangipane was once perfumed with the extract, though we are a long, long way from Bakewell.

There are few perfumes I would call hypnotic – tuberose, Casablanca lily, jasmine perhaps – but frangipani is up there with them. I go back to my room, head throbbing, drunk on flowers.

A café menu in Kyoto, each dish illustrated with a hand-drawn cartoon, narrated in detail on torn scraps of paper, glued scrap-book-style into a small leather folder.

Ful in Tehran

The traffic is bonnet to bumper, our yellow taxi so stuffy we must travel with the windows open, letting in thick grey fumes. A cacophony of horns and scooters jars on our nerves, the roar of motorbikes. Hand-pulled wooden carts rumble and squeak, there are big dogs locked in small cages and skinny, roaming cats. Shops selling rope or tin kettles, bread or tired and broken electrical goods. There are some whose purpose is a mystery. Everywhere there are men. Old men on pushbikes and young ones packed two or three at a time onto mopeds. Ancient men with shopping bags dice with death trying to cross these crazy roads. There is not a woman in sight.

We pull up under a tree at the side of the road, shoehorn the car into the only gap, inch by juddering inch. We pile into a café with dirty windows and smeared Formica tables, the sort of place you wish you had brought your own cutlery. Blue-plastic bread baskets are put down on the table by disinterested waiters. We tear off pieces of warm, ribbed flatbread. Fans whir on the ceiling, making not the slightest bit of difference. Plastic bottles of water appear and we wait for our order.

Everything we try to order has been met with 'yesterday' or 'tomorrow' and we make do with rice, stained yellow and orange with saffron, and a tepid and delicious stew of brown and pink beans, the first of many.

Wild berries in Lapland
Finland

It is late afternoon, darkness is falling and a stall in the town square is glowing like a candle. Tiny punnets of bright-orange berries on the twig – sea buckthorn – and jars of cloudberry jam jostle with honey and crimson lingonberries. I will not carry jars or bottles in my luggage, but I pick up a couple of cartons of berries to eat raw.

Buckthorn lives true to its name, and after a few minutes of parting the berries from their branches my thumb feels like a pincushion. I pick up a pocket-sized jar of jam and the fruit is tart, extremely so, and therefore right up my street. I nibble the berries as I walk. Cloudberry jam, in common with most berry preserves, has too much sugar for me but it is good too, bright-tasting and sharp. I will bring it down at breakfast tomorrow, to eat with Lapland yoghurt.

The buckthorn jam is pleasing, though not enough to risk bringing a jar home in a suitcase. It does keep a little of its acidity when simmered with enough sugar to make it keep. That is probably why it works, like damson, blackcurrant, plum and gooseberry. The more tart the fruit, the better the jam.

I arrive home after an exhausting long-haul flight. The garden is full of snowdrops.

Making home

Knowing where you stand

The land on which my home sits was originally woodland but was converted to pasture in the early 1700s by the Guidott family. The meadows provided grazing for the cattle that supplied much of the city's milk and cream. The farmhouse was known as Cream Hall and it is here that city dwellers would come to take tea – the farm was renowned for its cheesecakes – and in 1740 a Cake and Ale House opened 'offering cakes dipped in frothing cream, custards and syllabubs'.

The ale and cider used to make the syllabubs was brewed locally and may well have been the area's downfall, as it was not long before the farm and tea rooms became a thriving pleasure gardens where Londoners would come for dinner and to be entertained by acrobats, musicians and firework displays. Grazing cattle and hedgerows had been replaced by jugglers, dancing and hot-air-balloon ascents.

By the late 1800s the pleasure gardens and sedate tea and cheesecake trade had taken a turn towards more debauched activities with 'drunken and riotous orgies' and became famous for parties and prostitutes. Even the city's most celebrated sex workers such as Cora Pearl were known to have attended events there. The area once famed for its cheesecakes had become better known for its tarts.

On a quiet, grey Sunday morning in February, when the world outside seems a little dull and staid, I take a certain pleasure in knowing that on this very site there would have been 'riotous orgies' going on. Nothing like that here now, of course, although I do regularly make a cheesecake or two and I did find a pair of knickers in the bushes the other day.

Making a kitchen

The house had a granny flat but no granny. The kitchen was long and skinny, too cramped for a table and chairs. The study window faced a blank wall and there was no larder or place to store kitchen and gardening kit. The cellars were dripping-wet and it finally dawned on me that, for all its fireplaces, magnificent drawing room and walled garden, the house I had just bought didn't really work for me.

At the bottom of a flight of worn stone stairs, the granny flat had two rooms, a kitchen and shower, and was used only for the occasional house guest. It was bigger than the flat I had just sold. It occurred to me that this space would probably have been the original, below-stairs kitchen of the house, that what was now the granny's kitchenette is likely to have been the laundry and that the shower room would more likely have been a larder than the bathroom it is now. I scribbled a plan in pencil in my notebook, and then another in ink.

The listing of the Georgian house, my tight budget (there was little or nothing left after buying it) and my own respect for the history of the property put paid to my dreams and drawings and the plan was shelved for a year.

The awkwardness of the layout for modern living continued to haunt me. It was by chance that I found myself in a neighbouring house, almost identical to mine and owned by an architect who had, rather sympathetically I thought, brought their property up to date. The clutter of small rooms downstairs had been combined into a long, light kitchen with room to cook and eat, a big, busy family room. If it could work here, then why not in my own house?

I interviewed several architects, some of whom were out of my budget, others I felt who lacked respect for the property and should never be let loose within a mile of a listed Georgian building. But one plan stood out, to both me and later the planning department, the architect pointing out that we were simply returning the kitchen to its original use and location. Better still, he discovered that two historic kitchen fireplaces lay sleeping under the plasterboard.

The winter of 2009 was particularly long and wet. The thick concrete floor had to be dug out, an unbelievably noisy and dusty job. Its replacement, of reclaimed York stone, arrived in driving sleet the day before the Christmas break and had to be brought flag by stone flag down flights of treacherous stairs in the freezing rain. To add injury to insult, I twisted my ankle walking on planks laid over vast holes that would house the utilities. My bank account dwindled perilously close to bankruptcy.

I was blessed with builders who were used to properties of this age and genuinely cared about the details, meticulously looking after every piece of lath and plaster; who used traditional materials and looked after every last brick. Slowly, steadily, I started to see how the house was going to work, and essentially the space in which I would cook, eat and write. An unworkable clutter of redundant rooms turned into a light, generous space, its adjoining storerooms and thick stone shelves put back to use and its lost fireplaces found and set ready to light.

Enchanted by the arrangements of pots outside people's front doors in Amsterdam. Some sophisticated – an acer, a tobira and a flowering thyme. Others random, a higgledy-piggledy cluster of plastic pots, plants both dead and alive.

Choosing paint

The distant pftt as the envelope comes through the letterbox and lands on the doormat. The quiet excitement as you pull out the new colour card. A thing of beauty, each rectangle hand-painted in shades of toast, muffin, mushroom cap and fern. I rub my fingertips over the paints, feeling the thick brushstrokes of ghost and parchment, linen and blossom. Could this, finally, be the right one? Yes, yes, this is it.

The wait for tester pots or large sample cards feels like an eternity. The doorbell, the little carboard box of paints, each pot the size of an eggcup, a little pot of hope. I find something with which to prise off the lids – the oyster knife will do. If not, then a dinner knife. The chopstick I use for stirring is pulled from its home under the sink, likewise the narrow paintbrush, religiously washed after each batch of samples.

I discard the pot that is clearly a mistake, nothing like the colour card. My brush goes into the one that will most likely change my life for the better. The paint is like velvet, like dipping a toast soldier into a soft-boiled egg. I paint over the sheet of card, stroke by stroke, calmly, generously, then put it to one side to dry. I move on to the next. Within fifteen minutes the work surface is covered with sheets of freshly painted card, each one a minuscule shade away from the other.

I start a second coat, even though the first isn't quite dry. I long ago gave up on the better-known paint companies' offerings, whose PR is as glossy as their paint, whose names range from quaint to downright daft.

And in truth, no matter what silly name they give their latest shade, all the paint has an underlying back note of green.

The truth is that the colour is less important than the texture. It is the sheen, or lack of, that really matters. The actual colour will depend on the light in the room, the colours outside the window, the type and wattage of your bulbs, the time of day and, it has to be said, your mood. There is no point in going to the paint store with a tear-sheet from a magazine as that photograph will have gone through so many processes before it gets into your hands. Likewise, a picture on the internet.

You could measure my life in tester pots. Even now, when I know many of the artisan paint companies' owners by name, when I can picture exactly what a paint colour will *really* be like on the wall just by glancing at it on the colour card, the excitement of a release of new colours never dims. So roll on, silly names.

A larder – at last

I had always wanted a larder, the walk-in food cupboard I had known as a child, with its marble shelf where the remains of the Sunday roast – a chicken or a leg of lamb – lay on an oval serving dish under a tea towel and where there was always a cake in the cake tin.

Moving into this house was my first opportunity to create such a space of my own. My previous kitchens had themselves been barely bigger than a pantry, but here were several small rooms in the basement that could be repurposed. One, a gardening cupboard with thick stone shelves suggested itself, but its position next to the boiler room made it too warm and there were holes in the brickwork, which would surely make it a haven for mice. I settled on converting a small, stone-floored room that was, at the time, a shower room. We ripped out the pipework, plastered the walls and inserted a white marble slab. We lined the walls with narrow shelves just wide enough to take rows of storage jars and screwed iron hooks on the wall and the back of the door for shopping bags and a linen potato sack. A tiny wine rack was installed against one wall and there were tall shelves for the largest of glass storage jars.

The day I filled my little larder with jars of beans and seeds, sugars and flours, was one I had looked forward to all my cooking life. A little space for tins of sardines and bottles of anchovies, a dark corner for dried shiitake and porcini, and a home for tins of treacle and golden syrup. There was an entire shelf for vinegars, a tall one for bottles of rose and orange blossom water and shallow ones for slim boxes of crystallised violets and jars of candied orange and citron peel. Two pink egg cartons sat on the marble slab along with space for pots of marmalade and damson gin.

Over the years the larder has changed a little, and I soon realised I needed to make space not just for dried beans (flageolet, cannellini, ful, chickpeas, chana dal, green and brown lentils – I could go on), but also for bottled and tinned. Dried fruits now take up eight storage jars and there are at least six of rice (white and brown basmati, arborio and pudding rice, sushi rice and a Spanish rice called bomba that makes a delicious paella and produces a fine undercrust). My obsession with storage jars is a result of a personal concern over opened cellophane bags of ingredients in the cupboard, bags that fall or unfold allowing the contents to spill or spoil.

You can often tell the time of year by peeping through the larder door. At Christmas I juggle jars and bottles to make space for be-ribboned packages of panettone and Stollen, golden tins of Lebkuchen and the muslin-wrapped Christmas pudding. In summer the marble slab is a useful space for ripening peaches and melons.

One thing I have dithered over is the nomenclature of this infinitely useful space. Historically a larder was a cool place where you would store preserved meats, hence the name, the joints of meat and poultry hidden in crocks under a deep layer of lard or duck fat. Pantry denotes a dry store for bread and dry ingredients kept for the winter. Yet larder it is, possibly because I secretly hanker after a room filled with earthenware dishes of duck confit and fat-shrouded terrines, rows of knobbly salamis and sides of salted pork hanging from a hook on the ceiling.

Once again I get out a bottle of plum wine, the Japanese umeshu, pour the liquor over ice into a favourite glass and accompany it with a couple of dark-chocolate orangettes.

Kit

A pot sits next to the stove. Made of Bornholm clay with a glaze of clear ice-blue, it is home to my most-used kitchen kit. The humble edit of wooden spoons and spatulas are those for which I reach without thinking. A collection honed over the years to include only the barest of essentials, the tools that have earned their place next to the cooker. Each piece is a pleasure to cook with.

They are valuable only for their usefulness; reliable and solid, each with a clear purpose. A deep-bowled elm spoon; a brass spatula speckled by heat with which I turn a courgette fritter or pork steak with such ease; the simple Japanese steel tongs from which I never wish to be parted; a slotted slice made of walnut wood whose edge has darkened from years of scraping at caramelised meat juices. These are the kitchen pieces I work with more than any others, the most basic tools of my trade. It is a privilege to cook with them.

Without exception each piece is hand-made, possessing the fingerprint of the carpenter, spoon-carver or metal worker who made it. This odd collection has all the notches and furrows, scorch marks and stains that come with daily use. They bear the scars and well-worn edges of pots stirred and dishes cooked. This cook knows their every crack, crevice and dimple. Put them one by one in my hand and I will tell you what it is with my eyes closed.

The vegetable peeler that lived in the pot went missing in action long ago. Cheap, as old as time, never once did it ask me to sharpen its skinny blade. I still wince that I could have so carelessly chucked it out with the potato peelings. Heartless man. A little bit of me wonders if, like my missing antique silver teaspoon, my old peeler will one day come home. 'Have you missed me?' it will say as it eyes its precision-made replacement with the non-slip handle and laser-sharp blade. Sharp and capable of effortlessly skinning even the toughest celeriac or parsnips, yet nothing to which you could ever get attached or even particularly enjoy using. Essential, efficient and precise, yet totally devoid of spirit.

Just as a carpenter has his favoured chisel, these pieces of wood, brass and steel feel right in the hand. They work for me, though possibly no one else. They are a vital part of this kitchen and of me.

Six white-shelled eggs, stamped with green and pink in a green egg carton. As pretty as a box of fondant creams.

Knife, fork and spoon

My cutlery, the knives, forks and spoons in use every day, is left unpolished. The patina that develops over time, the subtle shades of misty silver, amber and copper that build gradually, lend a beauty to tableware that cannot be successfully replicated by manufacture. Old, tarnished cutlery whispers its history, its sparkly quality subdued by meals enjoyed. The baptism of time. By contrast, glistening cutlery that has been newly polished seems cheap and shiny. What I call shouty.

I long ago replaced my washing-up bowl with one made from glazed earthenware. A pale greeny-blue, it is more pleasing to me than the plastic variety.

A pile of plates

Inside the old cupboard to the left of the kitchen fireplace you will find several piles of plates. White, cream and celadon plates, ice-blue and soft-grey plates. Old plates and new ones. Plates the colour of old parchment. Plates from Korea, Japan and Scotland, Denmark and Greenwich. Tiny plates for cake and deep ones for soup. A large, pale-pink plate for a pale-pink cake.

Some of the glazes are crackled, like ice on a pond. Here and there are freckles and smudges of magenta from a blackcurrant tart or a beetroot salad, or yellow from a turmeric-scented pumpkin curry. Some are chipped or cracked, others have seen better days. No two match, though they all sit comfortably together, a happy mix of fondant-coloured porcelain, or blue-and-white freckled salt-glazed earthenware, waiting for tea or dinner.

Potters tell me they are not fond of making plates. Plates are prone to warp and twist in the kiln and take up the space that could be more profitably used for cups or bowls. The contours of a twisted bowl are much admired, a plate that isn't flat less so. A couple of my plates were salvaged from a sunken shipment of Chinese porcelain. They are the colour of the sea and still sport red wax seals on their undersides. I would love the maker to know their work wasn't lost for ever.

Not one of my plates carries a maker's name. Just the gentle bumps and ridges, dimples and hollows from their time in the potter's hands. A few sport the potter's mark, a subtle, often faint note to identify the hands that formed it on the wheel, glazed and placed it in the kiln and fired it. The plates are never really mine. They will always belong to the hands that made them.

I choose a plate from the pile with much thought about what it will hold. Will the food look lost or a little too snug? Will dinner feel comfortable with that hue of glaze? Such considerations were originally instigated by my job, where everything I cook is also photographed, but they have now become as much a part of life as choosing what we will drink with our dinner. There is delight in selecting a plate, even if it is for yourself. Better still is picking one for someone else, something quietly perfect to hold sustenance you have made specially for them.

At a café in Tokyo I order cheesecake. It comes in a thick slice with a lightly caramelised crust in the centre of a small white plate, the glaze gradually darkening to a deep cream towards the middle. To the top of the plate is what at first I take to be a logo, a golden crest. It dawns on me as I eat and sip my tea that it is in fact a carefully mended crack. A delicate piece of kintsugi, an exquisite golden repair.

A white plate

Occasionally, food can look most tempting when it sits on a simple white plate. Not, I think, a box-fresh white plate with a cold and painfully shiny glaze, but a white plate that has had something of a life. When the glaze has dulled and crackled over time; where years of knife-and-forkery have left minute scars and scratches and the surface bears the marks of decades of dinners enjoyed. Such plates have a natural warmth and familiarity to them, earned from years of use.

I picked up another old plate today, from a charity shop. A well-used plate with a single letter M on its rim, the stamp being the signature of a now-defunct restaurant. The china must have seen a thousand dinners and diners. Who knows whose knife and fork may have graced that plate or what business transactions or delicious gossip it may have overheard. I say that because the restaurant was very fashionable in the 1950s, frequented by much of London's glitterati.

A piece of fish on a plate whose rim is lightly scalloped, perhaps with a beurre blanc sauce, the sort of thing you can still find in Paris if you look hard enough, can be a quietly perfect thing. In Milan or Florence, a handful of chewy, egg-shaped gnocchi on a thick, time-worn white plate is probably more my thing. These are dishes whose simplicity and history beg for the most basic of white porcelain, with not so much as a simple dark-red keyline or a single crest to detract you from the food's calm, understated perfection.

I'll have a pork chop and a slick of apple sauce on mine, please.

An honest pot

Grey, unglazed stoneware, rough to the touch with the occasional ridge round the top. A simple button handle, quite perfect. The two handles are integral, pulled from the body rather than separately formed and attached. They feel secure as I lift the casserole and its contents from the oven. A single stamp near the base shows the legend of the Leach Pottery in St Ives.

Lift the lid of this plump, rounded pot and the glazed interior is the soft grey-green of a sage leaf, faintly crackled by time and heat. There may be white beans in a gravy of onions, thyme and red wine; there may be layers of sweet potato and dun-coloured lentils or in autumn a plump pheasant simmering with mushrooms and rosemary.

There is not one detail of this casserole that is unnecessary. Unadorned and functional, this is a quiet pot in every sense, no pop and sizzle to hear – you cannot use it on the hob – just the occasional murmur and sigh from the oven as meat exudes its juices, vegetables soften and caramelise, aromatics work their magic.

If I hadn't been a cook, I would have liked to have trained as a potter. There are parallels. You make a bit of a mess, knead and shape stuff, then bake it.

In the broom cupboard

Come to think of it, my family has long been obsessed with brooms. My aunt's upright wooden cupboard in the garage, emerald-green paint outside, yellow within that smelled of creosote and Izal disinfectant. Our cottage, whose brooms were kept next to the rabbit's cage and bales of straw, each one's bristles as neat as a whistle. My own broom cupboard's origins are a mystery, a cosy, brick-walled room with a fireplace and hooks from the ceiling, suggesting a drying room for the household laundry or perhaps somewhere to smoke a kipper. Whatever, it is now home to my collection of brushes and brooms.

A long broom for the stone terrace, its bristles as stiff as a colonel's moustache, so strong it will weed the cracks as you push. A soft white-bristled 'butler's broom' to tease errant crumbs from the dining-room floor and a small 'deck brush', like a nail brush on a stick, which is good for the grouting on the wet-room tiles. And then there are brushes bought out of obsession, the right tool for the right job – a long, skinny brush that slides neatly in between the staves of the radiators; an ostrich-feather affair, camp as Christmas, whose gorgeous feathers swoosh dust from the pelmets. Except that this house has no pelmets.

Hanging from one of the iron hooks is a cream canvas bag – a squirrelled collection of wooden-handled bottle brushes and washing-up brushes. I buy them in a cluster from old-fashioned ironmongers. (I have an unnatural hatred of plastic washing-up brushes.) The room smells of soot and shoe polish, almost certainly from the chimney, which probably needs a visit from Nigel the chimney sweep (no relation) even though it hasn't been used in decades. My spiky collection now shares its home with a giant gas boiler, which is deeply unromantic and frankly terrifying.

There is beauty in a hand-made brush. The patina of the wood, beech or elm, the neat stitches that hold the bristles on the head, the feel of the horse or goat hair against your hand. The fat 'dust-pan' brush has bristles made from the hair of both the horse's mane and tail. It is fat and generous and soft enough to use even on emulsion paint without scratching. Others are here because I found them – their history and feel – irresistible: a book brush made with pear wood and the softest white goat's hair; a thin blind brush for the Venetian blinds I no longer have and a brass-bristled suede brush for the suede boots I do.

I have resisted brushes for parquet flooring and computer keyboards, but not the slim coconut broom, which is a boon for sweeping between the terracotta pots without moving them. I suspect my ownership of a hog's-hair 'room broom' is not so much for its everyday usefulness as it is because I simply like calling it by its name.

There is, however, good sense in this bristle madness. It is as satisfying to use the right broom for the right job as it is to use the correct tool in the kitchen. Like removing skin from a fish fillet with a pliable 'fish knife' kept almost solely for the purpose, or skimming froth from a kettle of jam with a fine-holed spoon, using a soft brush on a wooden floor or a set of tough bristles on a stubborn stain on the path is quietly satisfying to a homemaker. Well-made brushes last for years, if not decades, and make a horrid job strangely pleasurable. Occasionally they are also the only answer, as anyone who has ever tried to clean inside a bottle without the help of a suitably sized bottle brush may have discovered.

Those more brush-obsessed than I (yes, they exist) will delight in a special one for deckchairs (short, made of soft horse hair and beech wood) or for cornices and cabinets, cobwebs and clay pots. There is, however, an element of good sense in building up such a collection. Too hard a bristle may scratch your paintwork, refuse to bend into the curves of your banisters or tear your pastry. It may get wedged in the neck of a bottle or tickle rather than rough up your suede shoes. All I know is that getting the right brush has turned many a household job into a pleasure rather than a chore.

In Kurama, Japan. A little train, its carriages decorated with leaves and a fawn. Another with cherry blossom and a geisha.

The house of moths

The house has moths. Small, just a few millimetres from wing tip to wing tip, but whose larvae will happily chomp through a jumper. A favourite throw, the colour of pine needles, is as eaten away as a lace curtain; an old navy jumper – a dear friend – wears a row of five holes on the shoulder, and I cannot tell you how many other things announce to the world that 'here be moths'.

Truth be told, I do not mind. I like the idea of darning. Some have made it into an art form, and so it should be. Especially if the repair isn't hidden but completed in a complementary colour. Pale baby-blue on a black jumper, for instance. Deep pink on orange, whatever. A contrast that will show that the repair is not something of which I am ashamed but to be shown for what it is, evidence of care and attention, of frugality and respect. A piece of craftsmanship. Also, an act of defiance.

Three pairs of wooden geta on a large, smooth stone step. The shoes are so neat and evenly spaced they must have used a ruler.

A hand-raised pot

I am drawn to a hand-raised pot as much as I am to a hand-raised pie. By which I mean a pot made without the use of a potter's wheel (or, in the case of a pie, without a metal tart case).

The pot is shaped by the artist's hands alone, the clay pulled and teased – ushered – into shape. One of the potters whose work I admire and collect, Jennifer Lee, works in this way.

Lee works her pieces till the surface is as smooth as silk. I fancy she whispers to the piece as she works, using the ancient methods of pinching and coiling the clay. Some potters whose work I also admire look like they wrestle with it. But there is a quietness of spirit to her pots, no matter their size. There are no glazes, the colours are those that run naturally through the clay, in some cases clay that is aged for years, decades even, before it is used.

Despite their size, these pots have a small base, barely larger than a pound coin. Placed on a table or a shelf, each pot looks as if it is floating, levitated, almost ghostly.

Lighting the table

Each Christmas my parents would light candles for the table, flames that softened the twinkling pink lights of the tree and infused the air with the smell of beeswax. As the candles burned low into the late afternoon, their shadows hid the gaudy paper crowns and detritus of Christmas crackers that lay torn, their snaps exploded. The flames made everyone's eyes sparkle, the sugar crystals on the fruit jellies glisten and the edges of the room dim and more interesting. By five o'clock, instead of a scene of brightly coloured carnage, it was like peering at a fairy-tale world through a piece of golden gauze.

Candles are lit every day in this house: early in the morning to write by, and again in the evening by which to dine. The light thrown by a candle graces stoneware or porcelain, mutes any loud colours and makes every detail of a cup's glaze come to life. It creates shadows to amuse and delight the lone diner, or to provide blurred edges to the room when you are eating with family and friends.

Candlelight is convivial, creating a space that is warm and benevolent. As a child it meant Christmas; for this adult it means the start or end of another day. A candle flame illuminates the subtlest and most beautiful details of objects and people we love and successfully hides what we do not need to see.

A bunch of dahlias in a jam jar, bright as a carnival, on a polished zinc table.

The painting

I am standing at the till of the café in which I work, taking customers' bills and their money. I ask a long-standing customer how she
is and she replies that she is exhausted, trying to get a show ready
to open at her art gallery. 'You should come,' she says.

An hour or two later, a young man arrives with an invitation. My
first since the endless birthday parties I was invited to as a child. (I
only went for the cake.) The party is tonight. After work I wander
past the gallery. It is in an area in which I have lingered many times
on my afternoons off yet I have never dared to walk into any of the
galleries, not even to ring the bell to gain admission. I hang outside
briefly; the small space is crowded with tall, elegant people drinking from tall, elegant glasses. No one seems to be looking at the
paintings on the wall.

I run my fingers over the copperplate printing on the invitation in
my pocket. To everyone's left is a painting, the likes of which I've
never seen before. Small, in brilliant jewel colours, thick swooshes
of pigment so vibrant it appears the paint could still be wet. The
colours sing out against the dark night. Too timid to enter, I walk
away, thinking of the painting on and off for the rest of the evening.

A decade or more later, a dark winter's afternoon, I am drinking
tea in a tea shop and the woman to whom I once served breakfast
every day appears from upstairs. Surprised, we greet each other (I
am shocked that she remembers me) and I tell her about the day, a
lifetime ago, when I so badly wanted to come in but was too shy to
cross the threshold. 'We still have the artist's work,' she says, 'come
and look.' I follow her upstairs to a panelled room and there, on the

wall, is another picture clearly by the same artist, its swirls and gushes of paint glowing in the dim light. 'Borrow it,' she says. 'Take it home for the weekend and enjoy it.' I nervously agree and leave, the painting throbbing under my arm, wrapped in brown paper and string.

At home, I hang it on the wall and know instantly that the painting, with its deep, generous stokes of crimson, ochre and black, will never leave this house. And, to date, it hasn't.

A cluster of grey-bearded trolls stand outside a doorway in Helsinki, wearing tall red hats with pompoms.

The mouse

The signs were all there. The nibbled crust. The olive that appeared from nowhere. The gnawed parsnip. And then, as if to confirm my suspicions, the tiny black flecks, like nigella seeds that appeared in the cupboard in which I DO NOT KEEP NIGELLA SEEDS.

'Do you leave the kitchen doors open at all?' asked the uniformed pest control engineer, who had kindly parked his van further down the terrace. I replied that, yes, they were indeed open all summer, especially when I was cooking.

'Pots of rosemary and basil to hand; thyme within arm's reach and it allows me to keep an eye on the progress of the ripening tomatoes.'

'That'll be it then. He just popped in from the garden.'

That I wasn't to be charged for the executioner's visit, a bill of several hundred pounds, came as a relief, but not quite so much as the assurance that it was a one-off visit by a solitary, curious field mouse.

'We only charge for an infestation, not for the odd weekend visitor.'

That should have been the end of the tale.

I was, however, quite unprepared for the side effects the little bugger's visit would bestow on my well-being. From that day onwards, every shadow, stray leaf or abandoned potato peeling brings with it the renewed fear that he has invited his friends round. I cannot tell you how many times I 'see' another mouse in the kitchen. Usually at night as I'm locking up, or early in the evening when the kitchen is filled with skittering shadows from the wisteria outside. During the day, each dropped sesame seed now becomes a mouse dropping and every shred of paper or blemish on an apple is instead the sign of a little brown rodent busy at work.

In truth, most houses have a mouse. Maybe two. The owners, of course, deny this. But it is a fact that mice can wriggle through the smallest of holes – the size of a pencil is the illustration I hear most often – and that once you have one, then you will almost certainly have many more. Mice, apparently, only stop shagging in order to eat and defecate.

Despite the appearance of my mouse being a certified one-off, every cupboard is now opened in trepidation, each dried leaf that blows in as you open the door becomes an infestation, each misplaced crumb a sign ... that the mouse is back.

Finding a long-lost object at the bottom of a bowl you haven't used in a while. An incense holder or a billet-doux, a foreign coin or a faded Polaroid, a misplaced ring or a single tarnished paper clip.

The perfect tea towel

My collection of tea towels would embarrass a more house-proud cook. Many have holes, tears and loose threads. Some bear scorch marks from their double life as an oven glove. (A risky habit, but one with which I persist.) Yet I am curiously fond of them.

A cook needs a tea towel. A soft cloth for polishing a glass or for drying a bowl or a plate too precious to have taken a ride in the dishwasher. My tea towels are mostly white and made from cotton or linen and have stood the test of time. They are washed but never ironed, at least not with a steam iron. They are pressed by the magic known only to Aga owners, the method of neatly folding your towels then placing them in a pile on one of the chrome domes that cover the hot plates. The following morning, as you come down to breakfast, you will find that a small tower of perfectly ironed linen awaits you, not a crease or wrinkle in sight. It is as if your ironing has been done by fairies. I only wish they would do my shirts.

Some tea towels do not dry effectively. This is particularly acute in new ones that have yet to be washed because of a fine layer of oil on the cotton. Once washed, it will dissolve and make the cotton softer and more efficient at its job. This is why it is best not to use fabric conditioner in your tea towel wash. Something I wish I had known sooner. Fabric conditioner is basically oil that makes your clothes feel softer.

Most tea towels are made of linen. (Irish linen glass cloths are worth every penny.) Linen is especially absorbent and tends to leave less lint behind. Many swear by terry cloths as the threads are looped, therefore giving a greater drying area, but I cannot get on with them. They lack the clean, freshly ironed look of flat cotton or linen and remind me a little too much of the cloths they have on the bar in a pub.

The best tea towel is probably one you have had for years, the one that keeps on going, getting more pleasurable to use with every wash. Frustratingly, it may be one that bears some florid design, brand name or, worse still, a twee little poem. What matters is that it works. A tea towel tends to get better as it ages. Like us.

Note: I should probably point out that this is a different towel from the one I have hanging from my apron as I chop and stir and knead and peel. That is a kitchen cloth, a thicker weave, cotton not linen, and something I use to wipe my knife or chopping board during use. It is the cloth I most often use to hold a hot pan handle or to remove something from the oven. White, with a single blue line running along its length, its uses to a cook are endless.

Thirty-two pairs of gumboots at the entrance to a tiny ryokan in Kyushu. Each pair is neatly labelled in white paint in case it is separated from its friend.

The pot with the wisteria handle

Pear-shaped, with wide, faceted sides and a glaze the colour of wood ash, the teapot is almost permanently in use. It has a short spout like a seagull's beak and a handle made from dull-brown wisteria, wound round and round like a ball of tarred string. The lid has a circular, hollow knob, like a tiny, deep bowl. Made by Kyoto potter Noritada Kimura, it is one of two that I use interchangeably.

The pot replaced the dumpy Brown Betty teapot so beloved by the British, which, despite (or perhaps because of) its jolly round belly and shiny, tobacco-brown glaze, (whisper it) I always found rather ugly.

You can grow fond of a teapot. A daily reminder of family and friends, of chats round the table, moments of comfort and solace, of time shared with others. Unlike the dipping of a lone teabag in a mug of boiled water, making a pot of tea is the very essence of hospitality and friendship. Putting a pot of tea on the table will always be a gift, something with which to greet a guest or revive or reward ourselves.

It is why I could never live with an ugly teapot.

In Uji, a crisp wafer cornet of tea ice cream. A Mr Whippy of the deepest emerald-green.

The potter's mark

A row of pale, tall pots snakes across the uneven wooden floor of an otherwise empty whitewashed studio. It is 1995, the space is Egg, the small, discreet shop owned by Maureen Doherty; the pots are those of a young potter named Edmund de Waal. I open the door, tiptoe in, convinced I will step on a wonky board and send the whole show flying. I stare silently at the display of calm, still ceramics. 'Pick them up if you like,' comes the owner's relaxed response, 'hold them.'

Maureen's invitation to pick up one of the pots, to run my fingers tenderly over its undulating surface, to feel its shallow ridges and furrows, to hold its pale glaze, the colour of sour milk, to the light from the window – three, four minutes that were to change my life.

Maureen became a soft, guiding light. (I miss her style, wit, wisdom and inspiration more than I can say.) Edmund is a dear friend whose pots have been part of my home for many years.

Holding that pot changed how I look at every bowl, plate and dish in my kitchen. Is it a delight to the eye? How does it feel in the hand? Does it flatter the food? More importantly, does it enhance the pleasure of what we are eating and drinking?

Cooking food that is photographed, something that has been part of my work for forty years, had already led me to consider the relationship between food and what we eat it from. The warmth that you feel as you hold a thin porcelain bowl of steaming rice in your hands; the way your tea cools in a wide, shallow 'summer' tea bowl; the rightness of the food for the plate on which it sits. (Food must look comfortable on the plate.)

With one or two exceptions, I use all the ceramics in my house. If through age or rarity they have become collector's items, then so be it. The potter did not make, glaze and fire their work to sit in a glass case, but to be a useful part of someone's home. I feel bound to honour that. I hope that Lucie Rie and Hans Coper would be happy that someone still drinks coffee from the cups they made in their studio in the 1960s.

The exceptions are pieces that were made simply to be a pot. Not something from which to drink tea or sip soup, to hold a spray of blossom or to support an elegant twig, but to sit quietly, bringing calm and tranquillity to a living space. (Sometimes, a pot just wants to be a pot.)

I cherish the relationships I have with potters. Some are friends whose work I am lucky enough to live with, others are no longer with us but their life's work is and I am honoured to be able to look after it. I may have a potter's (or painter's or photographer's) work in my house, but I feel more custodian than owner. Someone to look after their pieces, to take care of them till they are ready to be passed on to someone or somewhere else.

I like choosing the right plate for the right food. A striped Cornishware plate for scones and clotted cream; a moss-green, rectangular platter for sushi; oysters from a round aluminium tray. There is no science behind this, it is purely a question of aesthetics, in the way that battered fish and chips 'tastes better' eaten out of paper or a Chinese takeaway does when eaten with chopsticks out of white waxed boxes than either does when tipped out onto a plate. It is why drinking a single espresso from a mug feels 'just wrong'.

My first tea of the day – no milk, ever – is taken in a pale, capacious ash-glaze mug. Its sides are thin, its nuka glaze the soft blue of the early-morning sky. Coffee will come in a dark, salt-glaze mug of deep greeny-blue. I drink my afternoon sencha from one of a small collection of tea bowls. I am a creature of habit, yes, but who honestly doesn't have a favourite mug?

Condensation on the underside of the lid of a black-and-gold lacquer soup bowl. The gilded cranes and willow branches look like they are speckled with dew.

The scent of a kitchen

My childhood kitchen smelled of warm ironing and wet dog, with Rak the golden retriever lying by the Aga to dry his soggy coat after a walk and my mother ironing my winceyette sheets. On the best afternoons I would arrive home to the smell of flapjacks, the comfort blanket of warm oats, sugar and golden syrup.

At the time of writing, a December afternoon, my kitchen smells of the crumpets just toasted. There are even better moments: quinces simmering calmly in their carmine syrup on a winter's afternoon, a dish of sweetly garlicky potato gratin or the cool, knife-sharp air of chopped mint. Those days when a batch of lemons have been grated for posset or curd or there is a pan of bubbling marmalade on the hob. The clean scent of cucumbers freshly cut for sandwiches on a summer's afternoon, or that of lamb sizzling and spitting on a barbeque and sending notes of thyme and garlic, smoke and charred fat into the air. At Christmas there is the hot muslin and fruit fug of a steaming plum pudding or soft fruit and brandy notes of baking mince pies.

Some days I want to bottle the smells of the kitchen and sell them: a just-baked blackberry and apple pie or basil being pestled for a sauce; the gin-and-tonic notes of juniper berries being flattened under the blade of a kitchen knife or lime leaves scrunched as they are tucked into a simmering green curry are smells I would pay for. On a winter's afternoon I will sometimes unscrew the lid of the cardamom pot or open the jar of vanilla pods and breathe in deeply. A trick I can also recommend for moments of inspiration.

There are also smells that are, I suspect, pleasing only to me and I have listed those elsewhere: snow, moss and old books, but there are others too: the watery smell of a freshly cut aubergine; the spicy notes of dahlia stems as you trim them for the kitchen table; a bread and butter pudding quietly browning in the oven, or that of a saucepan of rice puttering on the hob, occasional puffs of clove and cardamom-scented steam escaping from its tight lid.

Outside a grocer's shop in Kyoto. A box of miniature pumpkins and squashes, barely bigger than tangerines. Someone has gone through each one with a fine brush or perhaps a Sharpie, painting cute faces on them. Some are sleeping, others laughing. A pear-shaped squash looks surprised whilst a particularly plump one is puckering their lips. One of them is clearly being pleasured.

The tea bowls of Ryoji Koie

You can feel his fingerprints. The deeply incised cross, the energetic flourish that is the potter's stamp, the telltale abstract dents and notches, his extraordinary muted glazes, but there is more than that. No one leaves their soul in a pot the way Ryoji Koie did. As you twist the bowl between your palms, each curve and bump and furrow you feel is like holding one of Ryoji Koie's large, rough hands in yours.

If ever a bowl has spirit, then this is it. The Koie tea bowls are both glazed and unglazed, and some only partly so. Some are tightly cupped, the bowl deep to keep your tea warm. Others are wide and open – summer tea bowls – with a large surface area to cool your tea in the heat of the afternoon. I love the eccentricity and wayward energy of his work. There is no distinct style; many of his pieces are not easily recognisable as his, at least to my untrained eye. He was full of surprises and constant experimentation.

I like to cradle my tea in my hands without the hindrance of a handle, but a shiny glaze is often slippery to the touch. You can grip a Koie bowl. Many are rugged and distinctly rough-edged, but if you turn the bowl slowly in your hand you will find the natural resting place for your fingers. Ryoji was born in Tokoname in central Japan, a city of pots and kilns. He died in 2020.

Holding his pieces, as I do most days, I feel the potter's energy, his desire to experiment and why, though he respected Japanese traditions, he is often thought of as an 'enfant terrible'.

At the hot springs in Beppu, the water is so hot that someone has set up a stall in the courtyard where they boil eggs. You can buy them for your lunch.

The trays

In Mashhad, northern Iran, I am brought black tea on an aluminium tray. Battered and vast enough to carry six glasses of tea, a tin plate of flatbread, dishes of halva, feta and walnuts and a bowl of white sugar cubes.

In Bangkok, a shiny, lacquered tray bearing a single glass of iced water, the server elegantly bending at the knee as she places the drink on the low table beside me. And in Japan it is difficult to find anything, from a glass of sake to a shopping receipt, that doesn't come to me on a tray.

I live in a house of trays. Mostly wood, they reside in a deep drawer in the kitchen, stacked as neatly as one is able to stack flat objects of different sizes. I rarely want the first to hand, so the pile tends to spill as I tweak the required one out of its place. There are different trays for different occasions, from the tiny one-cup rectangular tray to the leatherbound rectangle large enough to host a three-course meal. There is a high-sided teak tray from a flea market; a highly polished lacquer version made in Kyoto and an oval fruit-wood tray with bevelled edges, English and much repaired, that came from a second-hand shop. There are others too, of polished chestnut and soft grey maple.

My collection is strange when you consider I previously thought the tray to be a rather naff piece of kit, the sort of thing to which I might finally relent when I am a chairbound pensioner watching afternoon television. The more I see them used in other cultures, observe how drinks and meals are arranged on them like a still life (we can go full OCD here) and the way in which they elevate even a cup of tea to something special, the more I look at them with respect rather than disdain. Tea made properly requires a tray on which to put the pot, the cup and the slice of cake. Coffee needs a tray on which to sit the accompanying cardamom bun, and even the early-evening drink needs space for the bowl of olives or rice crackers. A tray allows you to place and clear everything in one swoop. You make one journey, not three. It catches any spills from a glass or teapot.

Many trays are things of quiet beauty. The rust-red or black of Japanese lacquer is built up through months of painstaking craftmanship, layer upon layer upon layer; often they are at their most pleasing when the top coat of black finally wears and you see fragments of rust-red peeping through.

The trays I cherish most are the rippled Wagatabon carved from a single piece of chestnut or maple and whose surface has been gently furrowed by a craftsman and his chisel, a dying art. They have been made since the seventeenth century, yet you rarely see them. Nothing looks more at peace than a glass or bowl on their undulating surface, but you would be wrong to think the carved ripples are without purpose. Their presence grips your glass tightly, like the rubber on a modern waiter's bar tray, keeping its cargo in place as they move from counter to table. Beautiful and useful. William Morris would be happy.

Climbing into the cab of a combine harvester to plough a field of wheat for a television show. No one has yet asked me if I can drive and it looks so much fun that I would lie even if they did.

Two hands are better than one

The photographer wants to move a pelargonium into shot, my oldest, the one whose leaves smell of roses. The one that sits in an old and much-cherished terracotta pot. I watch in horror as his young assistant picks up the pot by its rim with one hand rather than two. Posing for the photograph, helpless, I see the rim snap and the pot crash to the floor in pieces. I pretend it doesn't matter. It is just an old pot. But it does matter. That old pot, hand-made a hundred years ago, would still be here if the thoughtless assistant had used two hands.

If you watch closely, other cultures use both hands where we would so often use one. In Korea and Japan a plate, a bowl or an item of clothing is most likely to be picked up and given to you using two hands. When you pay your bill, your credit card is returned to you on a little leather tray, again held on both sides, like an offering. It is as if everything, no matter how humble, is treated with respect. When you hand someone a plate or a cup with both hands you feel as if you are handing them a gift, an offering, which of course you are. It is also how things end up not being broken.

Scotland. Soft-grey sky. Beautiful rain. A silver chafing dish at breakfast of black pudding and another of haggis.

The chopping board

The chopping board is my potter's wheel. It is where things take shape. Its worn wooden surface is where I knead bread dough or roll pastry, it is where I slice a green bean or peel an apple for a tart. It is not where I chop onions or slice garlic, both of which are done on a smaller, thicker board that can go in the dishwasher.

To view my chopping boards, turning them over in your hands, is to read the palms of a hand, showing the wrinkles and scars of a life at the stove. They, too, hold a history in their notches and cracks, fissures and holes. They arrived pristine, made from the heartwood of the tree, washed and immediately dried so they would never warp and kept away from the aromatics that do permanent damage, the garlic and turmeric, fish and blood. Yet soon they became used for everything and have the telltale whiff of work accomplished, as if to prove their usefulness – much of which disappears when they are given a firm scrub with a stiff brush, as a Korean masseur might scrub his clients before massage, then, like them, the surface is lightly oiled, rested and ready to start work once more.

The boards bear scars marking days, years and recipes. A chronicle of sorts. Pale-pink blotches from a summer pudding; pomegranate freckles; a lunch of roast beetroots. There are turmeric smudges, cherry splashes and some dark-blue dots whose provenance is something of a mystery. I have inflicted pain on this old friend too. A gash from a Chinese cleaver, scratches from a thousand kitchen knives, a scorch mark from a carelessly placed hot pan. And, yes, the piece of pale elm has warped a little from being left wet for too long after washing.

Most domestic chopping boards are too small. Hash a posy of herbs and inevitably leaves and stems fall off the edge. Slice an orange and rivulets of juice flood onto the kitchen counter. My board is sixty centimetres by seventy, which is room enough to chop but too big for the sink. It is scrubbed in situ.

The board is heavy enough that it sits still as I chop. Thin boards have a tendency to slide. A damp tea towel tucked underneath will steady the ship. In my book a weighty board is as essential as a sharp knife. Mine is twenty years old and gets a decent wipe each time I use it, a good scrub every now and again. It is left to dry standing up and only when truly dry is it put back in the cupboard, sandwiched between the cast-iron griddle and a baking sheet that keeps the wood from buckling.

Lifting the pale, gnarled board onto the counter feels like the start of something. A blank canvas. A beginning.

An old tree laden with walnuts in an apple orchard in Gloucestershire. The soft-green shells have cracked open; pale-brown nuts peep out.

Potters' dust

The fine layer of white dust on scrubbed wood. Bare shelves on whitewashed brick walls. Rows of patient pots on wooden planks – ware boards – waiting for the kiln. Potters' workshops smell of clay and tea. Potters like tea. I guess dust makes you dry. The dust, as fine as talcum, attaches itself to the hairs on my arm, my blue work jacket, my boots.

There is much to fascinate in a workshop: the oily smell of a mechanic's garage; leather remnants and abandoned silk threads in an upholsterer's cuttings box; the linseed and wet-paint smell of a picture restorer's space (sadly, not a woodworker's shop, the scent of planed wood being too strong a reminder of the loathsome Mr Oakley, our bully of a school woodwork teacher). Yet none is quite so fascinating as a potter's workshop. It is always an honour to be invited in.

There are cupboards full of boxes of jagged broken shards, archives of the potter's favourite pieces and notebooks full of sketches by the artist's own hand. The studios are sometimes freezing-cold and sweatily hot in turn; they are often draughty and few have even one comfortable seat and that is invariably covered in dust – potters' dust I call it – but they hold a curiosity for me, a picture of what might have been had I not turned my hand to cooking.

Looking at my own kitchen with its whitewashed walls and flag-stone floor, its pale celadon pots and plates and heavy wooden table, I feel it lacks the creative detritus of craftsmen's spaces. Too clean. It annoys me that an artist's mess – paint, clay, leather, wood shavings – can be so beautiful, both workmanlike and painterly, whilst the mess a cook leaves behind is, well, just a mess.

Gothenburg, a pastry shop's window full of gingerbread houses sitting on a bed of snow. Suddenly, I am in a fairy tale.

The writing desk

I often wonder where people write their books and letters and sometimes imagine them at work. As they sit at their desk, do they look through a window and, if so, what do they see? Do they have a modern office chair or a piece of mid-century Danish craftmanship, and is it upholstered or with a patina from years of adjusting their position? Perhaps they are surrounded by teetering piles of books, or do they have bookshelves, and if so what are those books? Whenever I see a feature about a writer's home it is their desk I look for, and clues as to what it was like before the stylist tidied it up for the picture.

My own desk is a rickety thing. A piece of Japanese elm with a wide grain, its surface a patchwork of ripples and waves, notches, holes and cracks. It faces a mirror, which some people say they find disconcerting, but I like the light the mirror gives, and the sense that the room, my study, is larger than it is. It is quite low and its legs are short, as I suppose befits a Japanese desk, and occasionally I crack my knees on it. That is when I think about having the legs made longer.

I wonder, too, what is on writers' desks. A typewriter perhaps, such as Alan Bennett might use, or a pristine MacBook? Which writers still use longhand, and are their desks ordered or do they have to rummage to find a stray notebook, piles of papers collapsing in their wake? What, I hesitate to ask, do they do with the ugly stuff – the printers and paper shredders and other modern eyesores? Do they hide them away in an adjacent cupboard, as I do?

I admire the writer who can work at a clean white desk, devoid of anything other than a box-fresh graphite MacBook, but I need to be surrounded by stuff. My stuff. (I could never, ever 'hot-desk'.) Most objects have been in place for years, and once moved you will see their outline on the wood, where the sun has faded the surface around them.

The bits and pieces with which I surround myself could be considered a comfort blanket of sorts, like the poor threadbare teddy I dragged round by its ear as a kid.

- A shallow washi paper box, a gift from its maker, Wataru Hatano, never moves. Artist and craftsman, Hatano works in Kurotani, northern Kyoto, the traditional home of this soft, deeply matte paper, where the mulberry trees that go into washi-making are part of the landscape. The soft charcoal colour of the box is achieved with layer upon layer of tannin derived from fermented persimmon. It is a box of treasure, where I keep my folding wooden ruler, brown Yama-guri ink and folding wire-framed spectacles. For some reason it also holds a sprig of dried roses from the garden, their petals faded to the colour of belladonna.
- A set of leatherbound notebooks, standing spine out, in peat, burgundy and chestnut to distinguish their contents.
- An old kiribako. The deep, brittle box made from paulownia wood and used for keeping your tea bowl safe, complete with its faded silk ribbon and brushwork calligraphy, now acts as a bookend to stop the notebooks sliding.
- It wouldn't be a desk without a lamp. A Danish one from the 1920s, its shade of deep-amber glass gives just enough light to read by. In the mirror it gives the illusion of being a pair.

- A brown suede pencil case with its assortment of fountain pens and worn-down pencils and a walnut-handled letter opener.
- A dog-eared manilla folder with a string tie that is never, ever fastened holds loose papers, bills and work in progress, and there are cotton and leather envelopes bulging with receipts and invoices.
- A camera in a leather case and three bottles of ink as beautiful as perfume bottles, whose colours – deep indigo, blue-black and grey-black – I stray between.
- There is a Lion-brand ring-bound folder, covered in soft ivory cotton, that holds whatever manuscript I happen to be working on. Right now, this one.
- A brown glass vial of bois de cade, the essential oil extracted from juniper wood. The occasional sniff as essential me to me as a cigarette is to others.

I wish I could say my desk is tidy, but then neither is it a jumble. An old leather folder with a brass zip has sat in place for a decade or so. Baggy and scarred, it contains a plump notebook in which I write everything, the odd postcard and notes scribbled on torn pieces of brown paper. The bookmark is a dried flower, which is just too precious even for me, but its present was an accident, a sprig that fell out of its short vase and dried to a crisp on the desk. Anything to hand – a postcard, a scrap of paper, a ribbon – gets used as a book-mark, including a dead flower.

Kitchen scars

My long kitchen apron, faded to walnut-brown from many washings, is stained with the magenta of a batch of damson jam; fingerprints of saffron-yellow turmeric and a blood splatter of pink from what I suspect is beetroot.

My wooden spoons are decades old, worn down at the tips from years of rubbing the inside of a pan, the bowl of each stained pink from making raspberry jam or terracotta from years of stirring ochre-hued sauces.

There are patches of blackcurrant on the sea-green damask of my table napkins, soft from years of washing. I bought them second-hand because of their exquisitely detailed embroidery, their entwined initials now undecipherable, twisted and curling like the tail of a Chinese dragon. They could tell a tale or two. Laps they have sat on, lips they have touched, fingertips they have wiped.

There are scorch marks too, heat stains, on the wide elm pastry board, the one large enough on which to roll a strudel; the ring mark of a sauté pan branded into a claro walnut chopping board and a burn on the oven towel I use in preference to the more usual oven gloves that make me feel like I am cooking with boxing gloves on.

Each of these stains and cracks, scorch marks and chips carries a certain beauty. They are the tellers of stories, the diary entries made by food and knives and pans, by heat and acid and pigment. The first knife mark on a new chopping board always feels like an injury, but then, as you work, more appear and the elm, oak or walnut starts to show its purpose and tell its own tale. Your oven gloves, bread board and cook's apron begin to take on their own blemishes, stains and burns until they acquire a workmanlike patina. Scars on our kitchen kit, like those on our bodies, are a sign of a life lived and something to be cherished.

Making raspberry jam on a winter's day with berries from the freezer.

A ghost story

The previous owners had been vague, I felt, as to why they put the house on the market so soon after moving in. The estate agent was only a little more helpful when he, jokingly, suggested they had 'probably seen a shadow on the stairs'.

The restorers, who set to work in the dead of winter, six months before I moved in, had mentioned several 'cold areas' on the landings and staircase, despite the central heating being on and finding no obvious draughts. 'I think one of the house's earlier residents is still here,' muttered an expert brought in to repair a length of plaster cornice.

I arrived, together with three ancient cats, on New Year's Day 2000. Moving from a one-bedroom flat, I had little furniture to bring with me, so the house felt spare, almost empty. 'Do you think anyone lives there?' was a comment I heard more than once from inquisitive passers-by. Renovations to the property continued. Hammers, chisels, paintbrushes and plaster mouldings lay strewn around the bare floors. I was surprised when a painter, a rugged man, built like a Victorian outhouse, admitted he was not happy to be left working in the house alone after dark.

One day, a restorer – a quiet and gentle Thai man – enquired if anyone had ever died in the house. I replied that it was very likely given the property's age. When I pushed him on the matter, he replied that he was 'just wondering'. Weeks later, when he left to return home, he offered the information that several times, when he was alone in the house, he had seen a woman dressed in white on the upstairs landing.

On returning from what had become an annual trip to Japan, I found that a kind 'house-sitter' had encountered not only the appearance of a figure at the foot of their bed but a middle-of-the-night tug of war with them over the bedding.

I clocked, silently, that this was the same room in which the restorer had seen the figure in white. I kept quiet. Add to this that a visitor to the house experienced a feeling of being 'touched' by someone as he opened the door to the airing cupboard, and I was almost beginning to believe them all.

I put much of these observations down to the decoration of the house, with the somewhat Dickensian glow from the old filament light bulbs against the deep-orange walls and the fact that the heating, a rickety and probably unsafe hot-air system, caused the bones of the old house to swell and shrink, creaking as it did so.

Truth told, I had never found anything remotely unsettling about the house. I was aware of its history as a Victorian slum and a Catholic hospice, when it was joined to the houses on either side. I was also aware of a blocked-up doorway in the basement, a false wall in the old laundry that rang hollow when tapped and an area of very thin wall on the top floor between the neighbouring house.

Then, a carpenter, who had been working on the house for a long time, started complaining of back pain. He visited a chiropractor, who offered help but then asked if he had been working on an old property. Bemused, he said that, yes, he had indeed been working on a Georgian house in London. He didn't mention the house's history as a hospice. The therapist then went on to explain that they felt his discomfort was due to the fact that he was carrying a hunched figure on his back. Perhaps someone was using him to leave the property.

The carpenter then asked, somewhat cheekily, 'Any idea who it is?' The chiropractor replied, in a hushed, almost reverential tone, 'It would appear to be a nun.'

A production meeting for a new series we are about to film for the BBC. James, chairing the event, is writing notes on a whiteboard with a blue marker. Episode 4, recipe 1, Puff Pastry Chicken Pasty ... Recipe 2, Butternut Squash Risotto ... Recipe 3, Nigel Freestyle. Which the team translates as 'makes it up as he goes along'.

A favourite cup

A freezing-cold January afternoon in Tokyo, the light is getting dim and I step into a café and order a cup of coffee and a piece of cake. What arrives at my table is extraordinary. Black coffee in a wonky brown cup and a single slice of cheesecake on a small golden plate.

The day is cold; I hold the cup in my hands purely for the warmth. The surface of the cup is rough and mottled to the touch, as if covered in tiny freckles. It feels like the skin of an orange. Its shape is off-centre, slightly skewed, very different from any cup I have ever drunk from before.

I look more closely. I can see that the handle is not straight but has been put on at a slight angle. It looks unusual, almost a mistake. As I pick it up, I notice that my fingers fit perfectly into the handle, as if hand and cup have become one. When I lift the cup to my lips the top is not perfectly round as usual but slightly oval, as if the clay has been squeezed by the maker. The unusual shape is curiously pleasing to drink from. It is far from the perfection of mass-produced china I know, yet there is nothing crude or coarse about its construction or finish. For all its uneven qualities, this cup is a thing of beauty. As if someone has rethought the idea of a cup.

I ask if I can buy it, a request that is politely but firmly refused, but I do find out the name of the potter who made them. I am surprised and amused to find that the cup and plate have been made not in Japan but in England, and in a studio not far from my own home. The potter's name is Steve Harrison, also known as the 'Mad Potter'.

My first piece of Steve's work was a salt-glaze cup, dark green outside, a more subdued moss-green within, with a wonderfully exuberant, curling handle. It is one of three I now have, used in rotation for my first coffee of the day. Steve and I first met at his home, where he invited me to see his studio and his work in progress. We chatted over tea and a slice of sponge cake made by his wife, Julia. And when I say cake I mean a deep, soft sponge filled with jam and cream. The sort of cake you so rarely see nowadays, but the one we really mean when we say 'cake'. We talked about his work, but also about how using a much-loved cup or bowl can increase our enjoyment of what we eat or drink.

I love, love, love my job. There isn't a day, not one single day, when I'm not grateful for it. Imagine a job that allows you to make a living out of making something nice to eat and then writing about it. Mind you, there's been a helluva lot of washing up.

On honeymoon

'Oh, I pity those who do not know this honeymoon of the collector with the object he has just acquired,' wrote Guy de Maupassant in the short story 'A Woman's Hair' in 1892. I have been on that particular honeymoon many times and no doubt will again.

The latest one started several weeks ago, in the back room of a London art gallery, to which I had been invited to view a series of raku bowls. (A rare opportunity to view the works of Raku Kichizaemon XV, whose family has made tea bowls on the same plot of land in Kyoto since 1586.)

Set amongst a row of sister pots, this particular piece whispered sweet words in my ear. I tried to look at the other works; indeed, I picked them up, slowly, carefully, one at a time. I turned them, tenderly, apprehensively, in my hands, feeling the imprint of the potter's hand. But in this particular piece I felt something more. My heart started to beat a little faster, I may even have broken out into a slight sweat. He had left behind more than a potter's stamp or a signature. He had somehow left his spirit.

As always, I asked for time. A futile gesture, as I already knew the answer and so did the gallery. (A pot either moves you or it doesn't, and I have no poker face to hide behind.) I felt slightly breathless, a little giddy, at the thought of acquiring this particular piece. This is a potter whose work I had admired, whose pieces I had travelled thousands of miles to see but had never been able to acquire. I had never before touched his work, never felt the roughness of the fired clay in my hand, never experienced the incredible lightness of his bowls or their brittleness.

The bowl has arrived and I lift it from its cotton bag with both hands. The box is wrapped in a coffee-coloured furoshiki, tied in a simple knot with a tiny artist's seal. I slowly untie the bow and open the cloth. The wooden box is wrapped in soft vellum and tied with a thick yellow silk ribbon. I unwrap once more and there is the wooden box, signed with the name of the bowl and the signature of the artist. The bowl is swaddled in silk the colour of sour milk and I unwrap it slowly, one fold at a time.

The bowl has been bought for a specific place, which is where I place it, to sit amongst friends, kindred spirits. (It is a long way from home and probably speaks about as much English as I do Japanese.) I never forget that we only look after things, we are only custodians, and the pieces will hopefully go on long, long after I am in my own wooden box.

This collector is once again on honeymoon, and something tells me that this time it will last for ever.

A shallow dish the colour of clotted cream, a scattering of raspberries, wine-red loganberries, redcurrants on the stem and wild strawberries the size of a child's fingernail, complete with tiny alpine strawberry flowers. Never has there been a prettier dessert, and not a recipe or a creative cook in sight.

The hands of a cook

I write a cookery book

Getting over mumps but still not well enough to return to school, I burrow down quietly in the kitchen with my Staedtler pencils and an artist's sketch pad. I draw a large, round cake, its surface studded with almonds, like a Dundee cake, then, pleased with the result, continue with a cup and saucer and teapot. Mum asks me why the cups are the same size as the pot. It is not meant as a criticism, but I take the comment to heart. I go over the pencil lines carefully with my fountain pen in blue-black ink.

Before long, I have my paints out too and not only fill in the outline of my Brown Betty teapot but paint cakes on a plate, their tops covered in pastel icing. I faithfully copy a cake recipe from the Aga cookbook my mother keeps in the bowl of the old Kenwood mixer.

I move on to a plate of salad, this time using brighter colours. There is no recipe, so I simply list the ingredients neatly in fountain pen under the picture. My beetroot is a rather lurid purple. I draw some lamb chops and a bowl of apple crumble (which is pretty much all I will eat at seven years old). Sunday lunch gets an entire page to itself. The morning becomes the afternoon and I am still drawing and painting plates of food, jam jars of poppies and a rather poor attempt at Rak, our golden retriever.

Miss Poole, the favourite of all my teachers, has just taught us how to sew (I proudly brought home a pincushion of pink-and-yellow sponge with a filling made from a pair of Mum's old stockings). There must be ten or twelve sheets of paintings and recipes now, some of which Mum seems amused by but I don't know why.

I sew the sheets together but get tearful when I find I have made my stitches so tight the pages won't open. We snip the red cotton with nail scissors. My book stays unbound.*

A train ride through Sweden. Vast silver skies, green-black forests. A tiny orange marzipan cake in my tuckbox.

* I can remember almost every page, though particularly the smell of the watercolour paints on the paper. In particular, the way the paint puddled and dried in different shades of blue and green. I was immensely pleased with this piece of work and it probably did as much to cure my mumps as the horrid medicine I was being forced to swallow. The book, with its painting, ink drawings and recipes, is long gone. It would have been my first cookery book.

Grinding cardamom seeds on a winter's afternoon

It is a pewter-coloured February day. I crack open a palmful of green cardamom pods, flick out their black-brown seeds, then grind them to a fragrant, gritty dust. This is something to do with a pestle and mortar rather than in an electric spice grinder – the essential oils are released less brutally. Time to inhale the singing, resinous citrus and eucalyptus notes. I grind the powder with sugar, like an apothecary mixing a tincture, then funnel it into an old jam jar. I screw the lid on tight, in the knowledge that it will keep its fragrance for a few days.

Cardamom, native to southern India, is used by the Arabs to flavour coffee, but to twist open the lid of the cardamom jar on a winter's afternoon is to release the ghost of Gothenburg. In particular its soft, chewy buns – the beloved kardemummabullar and kanelbullar of Swedish coffee shops. A spiced bun is what I pack when I go out for the day in a town or city that is new to me. If I haven't found a tempting place for lunch, or I walk so far I find myself lost and light-headed, a bun will stand me in good stead. The spice is invigorating. A favourite pair of boots, a map and a bun is a sound recipe.

Four in the afternoon, and Haga in Gothenburg is still shrouded in a cinnamon mist. A smell that will often lead you, as it will everywhere in Scandinavia, to knots and twists and bundles of dough laced with pearl sugar, butter and spice. There will be coffee too, a slow-drip pot to go with your sugar-frosted bun. I am here at Advent and there is a light powdering of snow. The daylight is fading fast. There are candles burning in the windows, lacy wooden stars hang from scarlet ribbons. The temperature drops. Everyone is wearing a woolly hat.

I met cardamom long before my trip to Sweden, a bag given as a gift from my hosts on a trip to India. Plump green pods, dry and papery to the touch yet as bright as wet pistachios. Their smell as piercing as my late father's Old Spice aftershave. Somewhere here – Delhi perhaps – is a marble-walled hammam whose moist air is heavy with the smell of cardamom. Time has blurred the location, but the smell is clear. Base notes of mushroom (the telltale sign of a badly tended steam room) with top notes of cardamom and dream-like clouds of scented steam that swirls, spook-like, from the filigree vents under the worn marble benches. I kept those pods for a year or more, using them sparingly, knowing I would never be able to find anything as fat and fragrant at home.

A cardamom bun is less sticky than the cinnamon-scented kanelbullar; more giving than the currant-freckled curls of the Chelsea bun, but just as much fun to unravel as you sip your coffee. You can spend a pleasing afternoon making a batch of buns. The milk-enriched dough is spread with ground spice, sugar and butter, sliced into wide ribbons then fashioned into an untidy knot. Each cook seems to have their signature tangle. The surface is speckled black and white, a gritty mix of caster sugar and ground cardamom. The salt and pepper of Swedish baking and my drug of choice.

Kyoto, Valentine's Day. A basket of currant buns in the shape of a heart.

The grace of accuracy

I weigh stuff. It is what I do. Putting butter or sugar, flour or choco-late on the scales or counting the eggs or teaspoons of spice – and writing the number down in a notebook – is the difference between cooking and cookery writing.

Making dinner at home, it would never occur to me to get out the scales, but working through a recipe that is to appear in print, a blueprint for others to work from, is part of the job. The amount needs to be neither a little short nor a little over. It must be spot on. The grace of accuracy. It is, technically, the heart and soul of my job, which is rather devasting when I would much rather think of that as a matter of art and poetry.

Still, the act of slicing a piece of butter, putting it on the scales only to find it weighs exactly what I thought it might is a curiously satisfying thing. One of life's tiny triumphs. Knowing I have written a recipe whose numbers produce a satisfactory result is a major factor in how I sleep so soundly. The thought of a recipe whose grams and teaspoons, litres and centimetres are wrong is almost certain to keep me awake.

Autumn lunch. Brick-red tomato soup. A single purple basil leaf.

A guest in my own kitchen

There are more guests than there are seats round the kitchen table. Even the dining table, a location used more for work than dinner, is too tight. (It is here that we lay out papers and proofs, photographs and props. The table's oak boards have seen more paper than pudding.)

The high-ceilinged drawing room at the top of the stairs, empty since I moved in, suddenly seems a perfect location for this rather large dinner. We borrow two trestle tables and a gaggle of velvet-covered banqueting chairs, stiff white tablecloths and Georgian-style silverware, a pair of candelabras and a side table for the waiting staff to use. With the lights dimmed and the candles lit, the room glows like Downton Abbey at Christmas.

I can imagine the parties this room hosted when it was first occupied as a private house or when it was home to a collection of Italian art (now at the Estorick Collection in nearby Canonbury and well worth a visit). And then I try not to imagine the room when the building was a slum, and the council issued a closing order on it in response to its squalor.

Tonight the room is once again filled with laughter, joy and friends' fierce appetites, but for once I am not at the stove. Margot Henderson and her team are roasting a leg of pork the size of a coffee table and a vast late-summer peach pie. As the evening goes on the chatter gets louder and more raucous and the room, briefly alive once more, feels like it should always be like this ... except that tomorrow, when the crumbs are cleared, it will return to its life of emptiness in a half-refurbished house.

Ancient varieties of vegetables growing under glass in the grounds of the Rijksmuseum in Amsterdam.

Stirring

Few kitchen moments are as peaceful as those spent stirring a fruit purée – damson, blackcurrant, plum – into softly whipped cream. The action, slow, deliberate but gentle, sends ripples of deep-crimson fruit through the clouds of creamy white dairy produce like rivers on a map. I give a fruit fool only one or two turns of the spoon. Stir one minute too long and the moment is lost and you have a bland, mauve cream. The crucial contrast between cream and tart ribbons of fruit purée is gone for ever. It is too easily done.

The cooking of onions in butter or oil is something you cannot hurry. They need to be stirred regularly as they make their way from being crisp, white and pungent to soft and sweet and pale gold. Today I need to caramelise them, a task over which I can lose the best part of an hour. I drift off as I usher them through the stages of sweetness until they are sticky and glowing like lumps of dark toffee. You can stop at any point along the route, depending on what you are going to use them for. Today they will be scattered over a yoghurt, mint and pomegranate raita, so I turn the heat up at the very end to crisp them too.

I cherish my quiet moments at the hob with a wooden spoon. Stirring porridge, custard or risotto is essential to the recipe: without the regular agitation of a wooden spoon, the mixture will scorch or curdle or fail to take on the appropriate texture. At other times I stir just for the sense of calm it brings. The repetitive rhythm has a tenderness to it, a gentleness that is in deep contrast to the slicing and chopping, searing and grilling that goes into making a meal. A meditation of sorts.

A spoonful of sugar

I have been given a jar of honey. It is becoming something of a habit. Jar after jar of the stuff. Just as others get gifts of home-made chutney or jam, I get honey.

Plump as a bee, pale gold and as thick as treacle, there is something jolly about a pot of honey. As presents go, a jar of the sticky stuff is always welcome. I twist off the lid and inhale. The scent today is of butter, toasted nuts and caramel whilst underneath lurks something dark, medicinal. A teaspoon is found and I dip in.

I like that first nip of honey, whether it smacks of fudge or chestnuts or something altogether lighter. I dream of finding honey that tastes of the orange blossom promised on the label. A pot of honey is a pot of memories, almost always good ones, as soothing as a Murray Mint.

But here's the thing. One spoonful is enough. Once that first hit has dissolved on my tongue, once the creamy, floral, buttery notes have dissipated, the second and third just taste of sugar. By the fourth I am wishing I hadn't started, screw on the lid and never touch it again until I need to make baklava or a batch of oat biscuits.

Few of my recipes contain honey of any sort, so every gratefully received jar sits there, sweetly sleeping, waiting for me to add it to a pan of poached pears or a cup of hibiscus tea. And yet I am always grateful to receive my gift, just for that first spoonful. That is truly the stuff of (sweet) dreams.

A single piece of glistening, pearlescent sashimi. A knob of wasabi and a sprig of purple shiso flowers, a rectangular plate the colour of moss.

Creaming butter and sugar

The radio is on, a documentary about Hinduism, the kitchen windows are fugged up with steam from our lunch of xiao long bao. There is a jam jar of horse chestnut buds on the table and I am baking a cake.

To my ear there are few more hopeful sounds than that of an electric stand mixer creaming together butter and sugar. A cake or a batch of cookies is on its way. This first part, the amalgamation of two crucial ingredients, is make or break for any cake.

The paddle smears the soft, pale butter up the sides of the bowl. The blunt edge sweeps the mixture round, spreading swooshes of fat and sugar over the shiny surface. Gradually the colour softens. If I am using light muscovado the hue will be that of a cappuccino. White caster sugar and butter produce a fluffy paste that looks like clotted cream. Use golden caster sugar and it will look like old parchment, the pages of an antique book. This is the creamy-white paper on which I draw, with golden egg and pure white flour, with chopped nuts and chocolate chips, ground ginger or purple berries.

Few recipe books tell you how crucial it is to get this right. If your cake is to rise, your cookies crumble tenderly in your fingers, then it is essential to mix and cream and beat and stir long enough for your two ingredients to become as light and whipped and soft as a Mr Whippy cornet from an ice-cream van.

I take my time.

An oval porcelain dish, eau de Nil, a faint impression of leaves round its rim. A tangle of pale sauerkraut, sprouted radish and purple chive flowers. A handful of scattered blackberries brings bursts of dark sweetness amidst the tart, fermented cabbage.

Baked plums and rosewater in Lebanon

I light the oven, a three-tonne beast attached to a gas canister, its black iron door adorned with hand-painted turquoise stars, the flames inside open to view. I run a small knife round each of twenty plums, pull the halves apart, loosen the stone with my fingers. The plums, yellow, claret and purple, are placed in a battered baking tin in concentric circles. A stained-glass oriel window of fruits.

I trickle wire-thin ribbons of honey over the fruit, the golden syrup pooling in the hollows left by the discarded stones. A lemon is squeezed into the dish, pips fall, the faintest puff of black pepper. I crank open the oven door with its carved wooden handle, then slide the dish into the furnace. The door clanks shut and we wait.

The fruits scorch in the fierce heat. The smell of plum jam fills the kitchen. Flesh bubbles, edges blacken, plum juices burst from their skins and mingle with the honey and lemon. Twenty minutes later they emerge, collapsed in a pool of deepest purple-red. I twist the lid from a bottle of rosewater, hand-made, no label, and shake drops over the scorched fruit. A scent of rose, sweet fruit and honey. We let the fruit rest for ten minutes.

The roasted plums are served on an old tin dish, a mound of salted labneh at their side, the juices seeping into the soft, thick yoghurt like lipstick into a pantomime dame's pancake make-up. I rain a pinch of dried rose petals over the surface and offer them up. We spoon the soft fruit and labneh into our mouths, then lift the dishes to our lips to drink the last drop of rose-perfumed juice.

There is a short row of cookbooks in the kitchen, tucked inside a cupboard close to the cooker. They have been much the same titles for years. Almost none of them still have their spines, and all are blotted and smudged with food and as well used as any chopping board or wooden spoon.

Making crumble

I am making crumble. Rubbing butter and sugar together with my fingers and thumb, mixing it with flour and a pinch of spice is something I have been doing since I first learned to cook. Crumble was the first pudding I made and I have been making it ever since.

The dish is round and shallow stoneware with a moss-green glaze inside. The crumbs are of assorted sizes, grit, gravel, pebbles and stones. I scatter only enough to provide a thin layer of cover for the fruit, so the crumble will split here and there, giving room for the fruit to bubble up in dark-crimson puddles and scarlet veins like roads on a map.

The crumble is a perfect pudding; the harmony of fruit is hot and slightly sour against the crumble, which is sweet and buttery. The balance of soft and crisp – I could leave it at that. But there is more, and better. In between the fruit and the rubble of the crust lies a layer where the two mingle. It is possibly the most desirable bit of the entire pudding.

Icing a cake

Some cooks pipe their icing through a cotton bag, its steel nozzle leaving exquisitely cut shells or dots, scrolls or rosettes in its wake. Like calligraphy, the art of decorating a cake where each squeeze of the bag is slow, purposeful and considered is one I can watch for hours, as if hypnotised.

My cake-decorating is more abstract. I pile most of the frosting, buttercream, icing, call it what you will, on top of the cake then rummage for the palette knife. An elderly wooden-handled knife, light and flexible, which I bought at Dehillerin in Paris forty years ago when I was at cookery school and whose handle now comes away from its blade. I draw the flat of the knife across the surface, pushing the icing into drifts and soft hillocks. I draw it back again to achieve a roughly even layer, then back again, this time with a swirling motion, as if plastering a wall.

Over the next two or three minutes, no longer, I continue to use my palette knife to produce creases, swags and waves of icing, deep and thick like drifted snow. No less considered than that done with a piping bag, but in a style that I hope appears effortless.

At Christmas the handle of a spoon or the softly rounded end of a table knife is used to pull up peaks, curved points of white icing that will stand stiff and hold a fall of icing sugar. For a coffee and walnut, a carrot and mascarpone-frosted cake, I will continue with my abstract swirls and tucks, the relaxed and gentle folds, like the sheets of an unmade bed.

The scarlet-orange of runner-bean flowers is joyful. It lifts the spirits. I sometimes wish I could buy them at the florist's and put them in a vase.

It started with a salad

We stand at our tables, smart in our new aprons. The class has torn its frisée into bite-sized feathers, washed and spun it dry in a wire basket and dumped it in a thick white china bowl. The chef, in full kitchen whites and a hat as tall and white as a wedding cake, instructs us in the manner of cutting pancetta into short, fat match-sticks he calls 'lardons'. We have fried them in a shallow black iron pan. The stubby chunks of cream fat and flesh the colour of dried blood now gilded and sizzling, we tip them onto the frisée.

I take the bottle of tarragon white wine vinegar and pour some of it into the hot, empty pan. The steam whooshes up, the fat spits and pops, the smell of smoked bacon, tarragon and vinegar fills the kitchen. I lift the pan a few inches from the gas and swirl it round, set it back on the heat, then scrape at the sticky debris left on the pan with a wooden spatula. I scrape at the toffee-like goo left behind by the pancetta and stir until it dissolves in the bubbling vinegar. The action reminds me of the way my mother made her gravy, scraping up the caramelised meat juices to enrich the liquid. I then tip the fragrant dressing over the frisée and toss everything together, the salty, smoky, knife-sharp dressing coating the frills and curls of the pale leaves.

Up to this point, I have thought of the salad and dressing as sepa-rate entities. You make a salad. You make a dressing. You toss them together. The idea that one should be enriched with the essence of the other is new to me. This is my first day at the Paris cookery school and in five minutes I have just learned something I didn't in two long years in hotel school in Britain. A crucial, basic thing.

It starts with salad, but the notion soon spreads itself throughout my cooking. From today, never again will I leave any toasted remnants of meat or vegetables in the pan. That goo, that savoury butterscotch, contains the soul of the meat, its juices, bubbled down to a sticky, golden nectar. Salty as Parmesan, as sweet as honey, it will never again remain unused. Never again will such goodness be left behind in the pan to be dissolved in the washing-up water.

Lining a cake tin

I am making a banana cake with light muscovado sugar and dark-chocolate chips. The first line of my recipe persuades me to line a cake tin.

I locate the roll of baking parchment and the scissors, place the cake tin on the paper and draw round the base with a pencil. My kitchen scissors carefully follow the pencil line as if I am cutting out a dress pattern. I take as much care to cut the shape accurately as I did when I was seven years old, tongue poking out, following the pencil line as if my life depended on it. I brush the base of the tin with melted butter and settle the paper in the base of the cake tin.

That done, I cut a piece of paper that will fit round the sides of the tin, making it deep enough to sit several centimetres above the rim in order to keep the top of the cake from burning. I snip a two-centimetre-deep slit every couple of centimetres along one of the long edges and both of the short ones, which will allow me to fit the paper into the tin neatly without creasing the paper. Failure to do so (I can be quite lazy) will result in creases in the paper, which also means creases in the cake. No one wants a creased banana cake.

I brush the tin with a little melted butter, then slide the paper into place. Lining the sides is always a bit more complicated than just the base, when the merest dab of raw cake mixture between the tin and paper will hold the paper in place.

Lining the container has probably taken me a full ten minutes of my life, but the result is a little work of art. Brown parchment cut to fit, neatly fixed and there to stop the cake sticking, but also to keep the cake moist over the next day or two. I could of course have used ready-made liner, even invested in a reusable one, but to do that would have kept me from the childlike joy of scissors, paper and concentration.

Listening to a cake

A cake talks. Lower your ear towards its soft golden crust – get really quite close, closer than you might consider polite – and listen. The more years you cook, the more you realise a cake cannot be cooked to perfection by watching the clock alone. A cake will tell you if it is ready or if it needs longer in the oven. You must listen carefully, for a cake can only speak in whispers. A cake cannot shout. Get close, and you will hear a low, soft crackle. Like that from the froth on a freshly poured beer. Your cake is talking to you and you should listen.

A silent cake is an overcooked cake.

When your quivering block of tofu comes in a pool of dashi and soy, a single pink cherry blossom on its surface.

Oranges are the only fruit

The first breasts I ever saw were on the tissue-paper wrapper of an orange. Partially obscured by locks of flowing hair, they belonged to a mermaid perched on a rock, holding a bunch of glowing fruit.

Not all my early oranges came wrapped in tissue paper, but those that did felt special, so much more so than an apple, almost exciting. Not every fruit in the wooden crates at the greengrocer's was parcelled up in paper, just a few and seemingly at random. Many of the wrappers, proudly showing the fruit's provenance as Spain or Sicily, Italy or Morocco, were adorned with pictures of it, its dark-green leaves and star-like white blossom.

Other wrappers became collectible for this six-year-old schoolboy and I would sit at the kitchen table, painstakingly unwrapping the citrus fruits from their snowy sheets, pressing out the creases firmly with my fingers, trying not to tear the fragile tissue. Although there was the odd image of duelling men, a spider and its web or a scarlet butterfly, most seemed to show women, many with long dark hair, sometimes riding a scooter, picking fruit from the tree or sipping a cocktail. Some wore bikinis, some not. My first stash of porn.

My collection of wrappers may be long gone, but not my reverence for the orange. I treat each fruit as tenderly as I might a peach and give it the same attention I did as a child, sitting every brightly coloured globe on its own plate, preferably with its leaf intact, sniffing its stem and hoping for – and occasionally getting – a teasing whiff of blossom. All that is missing are the teasingly illustrated wrappers.

Lifting the lid on a bowl of miso soup and hearing the almost silent sigh as lid and cup part company.

The magic of icing sugar

It is the lightest of snowfalls, the merest sprinkling of powdered sugar, but its presence, shaken through the mesh of a fine sieve, has brought a certain magic to the rugged surface of a tray of almond croissants. It has made a crescent of brown pastry and frangipane into a snow-freckled mountain range.

On other days I have seen icing sugar used as thickly as driven snow, on a tray of softly mounded walnut shortbreads or in the cracks and ridges of a Stollen. At Christmas, no Yule log or mince pie seems festive enough without it. Unfashionable, yes, but icing sugar brings a certain enchantment.

A dusting of powdered sugar can cover up a multitude of sins, but its presence is more than a way of papering over the cracks. It will highlight the crests and peaks of a crisp meringue, make a swirl of buttercream sparkle and render the deliciously blackened tips of a French apricot tart irresistible. When it lies on the waves and curls of a cupcake's piped frosting you would need a heart of stone not to be tempted.

My first encounter with this whiter-than-white phenomenon was in wooden boxes of rose and lemon Turkish delight, the pink and pale-yellow cubes twinkling in a bed of powdery sugar. I found myself sifting through the sugar to locate the short wooden fork that was tucked in to spear the grown-ups' answer to jelly babies. Later, I would use a dampened finger to retrieve the sugar that collected in the corners of the tin of fruit 'travel sweets' my parents kept in the glovebox of the car for long journeys.

The smell of home-made coffee and walnut cake.

The sadness of jelly babies

There is, if you examine it closely, an almost invisible dusting of icing sugar in the bodily crevices of a jelly baby. At least, that is what they are called now. Originally, in Victorian sweet shops the poor little things, sold alone without mummy and daddy jellies, were known as 'orphaned babies'. And this is where I admit to biting the heads off first. A bit *American Psycho*, but it is how I ate them as a child and how I eat them to this day.

The way damson stones float to the top of the pan when you are making jam.

Peeling an orange

I punch a slit in the peel with my thumb – the thick part at the top of the fruit, near the stalk. The cut near my thumbnail tingles. The zest squirts out in a single fragrant puff. The ghost of white jasmine-like blossom, glossy green leaves and running water. Tiny droplets sent airborne, an instant reminder of picking oranges in Marrakech, a hillside orchard in Sorrento, another at a villa on the outskirts of Tehran. (After a journey through the city's traffic fumes, an orange has rarely been more welcome.) I am not sure I would go scrumping for apples any more, but I will happily pull an orange from its branch, as much for the smell of its blossom as for the fruit itself. Most citrus trees bear blossom, leaves and ripe fruits at the same time, making for the most ravishingly beautiful orchards.

I tear the peel from the fruit in thick pieces, pulling away as much of the white pith as possible, going over it again later, tugging at the fine spider's web of pith that lives under the peel. I tear the fruit in half, remove the soft white core of pith from its heart (faithfully copied by Terry's in the now somewhat diminished Chocolate Orange), then separate the segments one by one, eating them complete with their white skin. The flesh is jellied and refreshing, but the skin slightly dulls its effect.

My brother, always something of a maverick, would halve his fruit with a knife, turn each half inside out, ravishing the flesh, tearing it away from the skin with his teeth, juice dripping down his chin. My father, more aware of the sofa's upholstery, would devour his on a side plate, first cutting four neat lines through the peel from top to bottom with his penknife, then pulling each quarter of peel from the fruit in a single piece, which I always thought a little odd until, some years later, I tried it. Maybe I should start carrying a knife.

Another whole fish at breakfast, this time black as treacle and stiff as a board. Entombed in what appears to be molasses and dark soy sauce, its mouth is gaping as if it died screaming. I feel as if any minute I might do the same.

Peeling an orange in the kitchen

Peeling an orange in the kitchen uses a different technique. Where you would have torn, you cut. Where the work is done with a blunt thumb, you use a razor-sharp knife. Rather than going straight to your lips, the segments end up scattered in a salad or the sauce for a roast duck. Each segment is vivid, blazing orange.

I roll the fruit back and forth on the chopping board, pressing down with the palm of my hand. Invariably this is a blood orange, whose skin is stippled and flushed with crimson. With my smallest, sharpest knife I slice a little cap from the stalk end, thick with spongy white pith. Then the opposite end. I turn the orange so that it sits upright, firm and squat like a barrel, then, holding it firm with my left hand, I go round the fruit, slicing downwards from the top to the base until all the peel is removed. There is a little pleasure in cutting away just the right amount of peel, so all of the white pith is removed but as little of the fruit as possible.

More of a joy than a job, the sweep of the knife as it follows the curve of the fruit is quietly pleasing, and if you have more than a couple to do, say for an orange salad, you can get into a rhythm that is almost mesmerising. The less fruit there is on your little pile of rind, the more satisfying the task becomes. Should there be any, then I simply pick up each piece of peel and squeeze it over the fruit, so as not to waste a single golden drop of the precious juice. A point that seems somehow even more important when peeling a blood orange.

At first I would slice too deeply, taking off great chunks of the brilliant fruit with each curl of pith, but then I got better at it. Once the fruit is shorn of its thick peel and pith, glistening with juice, I pick it up and cradle it in the palm of my left hand, then I slide the blade of the knife down between each segment of fruit, separating it from the gossamer skin in which it is encased. As the last segment of naked fruit falls into the bowl, I squeeze the flaccid ball of empty skins to press out the last drop of juice.

There is sheer delight at the bowl of peeled segments of fruit, each crescent glowing, a hugger-mugger pile in a moat of orange and rose-pink juice.

Fond as I am of matcha ice cream, today the Japanese go one better. What arrives at my table is two balls of vanilla with a trickle of matcha tea as green as wet moss on a rock.

Rubbing butter into flour

You cut the cold butter into rough cubes and drop it into the bowl of flour ... puft ... puft. Then you start to rub the two ingredients together between your thumb and fingers. The butter slides under your thumb, unrelenting at first, then slowly it forms into thin flakes, then breaks down into pebbles, then gravel, then grit. That is when I stop.

Many years ago, whilst working in the Lake District, I was told to look out of the window at the lake and daffodils below when making scones or crumble. 'Light heart, light baking,' I was told. The ideal texture of crumbs to top a plum, damson or gooseberry crumble is a mixed bag of all sizes, from specks of dust to fat lumps that will turn chewy in the heat. Occasionally, after adding the sugar I sprinkle a little water over the surface and shake the rubble from side to side in its bowl, so that some of the crumbs stick together in small pebbles. To do so introduces a more interesting texture than a uniform 'machine-made' crust.

The five minutes or so it takes to monotonously rub the ingredients together gives you time to think about other things, to drift away a little, but I don't. I like to keep a hawk's eye on every stage, to stop just when the texture is perfect, to delight in something so mundane, yet to pudding lovers a very important task indeed.

Whipping cream

You need a good whisk. By which I mean one with the thinnest of wires that swell out like a balloon. These are the ones that will beat air into your cream. A tight whisk with thick wires (there are plenty about) is best kept for stirring tins of paint.

I like to pop an ice cube into the wires; it helps to keep the cream cool but also melts a little, and your result will be lighter and more airy for it.

The first cream I whipped turned to butter, the achievement of teenage overenthusiasm. Nevertheless, it was piped on the tart of shop-bought sponge case, tinned fruit and Quick Jel glaze and eaten with a certain graciousness.

The trick is knowing when to stop. I can't tell you how many times I have got it wrong. The fresher the cream, the longer it will take. The higher the butter fat content, the quicker it will go from cream to butter. There is a point when the liquid cream starts to feel heavy on the whisk; you may think your arm is tiring, but your gradual slowing down is more likely to be due to the texture of the cream thickening.

How far you take it will depend on what you are using your cream for. (Though if the texture has darkened a little and the cream has turned grainy, you've blown it.) As an accompaniment to a slice of apple pie, the preferred texture will be on the soft, almost sloppy side, the cream barely able to keep its shape. For the filling of a cream sponge or a flaky cream horn (remember those?) it will need to be a little firmer, stiff enough to hold a shape. I test the texture by bringing up a soft peak with the blunt end of a spoon. If the cream will stand in a gentle mound, it is ready. If it slips back into a loose puddle then it will 'fall' and ooze once you have spread it on the cake or piped it into the pastry case.

The difference between the two is a matter of minutes, occasionally seconds. Which is why I slow down, checking after each turn of the whisk. You *can* use an electric whisk but, honestly, it is much more difficult to judge the moment to stop and far too easy to over-whip.

While I have you, can I make a plea for the return of crème Chantilly, the airy, very slightly sweetened whipped cream scented with the merest whiff of vanilla? It is gorgeous and as rare as hen's teeth. We made it daily at hotel school, just before lunch service.

You need double cream, a little icing sugar, the tiniest splash of the very best-quality vanilla extract or paste or, should you have such a thing, the seeds from a sticky vanilla pod (now almost the price of small family car) and ice. The ice is not an affectation. It is crucial to keep everything cool (which is why I start by putting a mixing bowl in the fridge) and its addition will lighten the cream to a fluff. As you whisk and feel the cream start to thicken, add a small handful of crushed ice to the bowl (about two tablespoons to a 250ml pot of cream) and keep whisking. Your cream will lighten and aerate. Once whipped, use it quickly, as it does tend to fall a little, and keep cream, bowl, whisk and the kitchen as cool as you can.

In Beirut, a vat the size of a dustbin filled to the brim with almonds, shelled but still in their golden skins; tucked amongst them are fat, rough ice cubes. A handful of chilled almonds, plump from the iced water, is replenishing, like drinking from a stream in the hills.

Toasting nuts

I take the pan, a shallow-sided affair that never sticks, in my right hand and warm it gently over a low flame. A handful of flaked almonds rains down on it. I keep them in a single layer – easier to watch their progress as they toast.

Nothing happens. The nuts sit there for three or four minutes looking exactly as they did in their jar, pale and uninteresting, almost devoid of any flavour. You need to toast a nut to release its flavour, not only almonds but hazelnuts and pecans too. As the flakes sit there in the pan, there is a temptation to get on with the hundred other tasks I have in my in-tray. Yet I know this story of old. Too many times I have been tempted away from the stove to empty the dishwasher or make a phone call, only for it to end in acrid smoke and blackened nuts. Once they get going, nuts burn in a heartbeat.

It is a change that happens in seconds and is almost entirely due the nuts' high oil content. A burnt nut is a bitter nut.

I keep my eyes on the almonds as they go from ivory to golden brown. They go through stages of cream, beige, fawn, toast, crisp-bread, tobacco and then, if I lose attention, charcoal. The colour is a good measure of their flavour. The mid-point, when they are pale brown, is where their deep roasted flavour lies. Once they have darkened beyond that their bitterness will kick in.

Patchy colouring is somewhat inevitable, but the trick to even browning is to keep the nuts moving as they colour. I tilt the pan from side to side, gently tossing the warm nuts, but without using a spoon or palette knife, which could shatter the brittle shaved nuts.

I toast almonds to scatter over cauliflower cheese or choux pastries; hazelnuts to add texture to a chocolate mousse; cashews for tossing with slightly too much salt to eat with a very cold beer. Walnuts are merely warmed, never browned, as they are apt to turn bitter sooner than the other nuts.

When making pastry, the way I dust the work surface with just the right amount of flour using one, and only one, flick of the wrist.

Wrist action

My success with making crêpes in Paris and my failure at appams in Sri Lanka is only partly down to the pan. A new crêpe pan or appa-chatti will cause your batter to stick, your work to fail. The older and more weathered your pan, the more chances of success, once it has built up layer upon layer of its own non-stick coating. The slippery surface that can only come with being used for the same thing over and over again. A surface that cannot be copied by manufacture, only by steady, regular application of heat and food.

But that is only part of it. A reliable recipe is a help. But just as much depends on the deftness of the wrist, the way you turn the pan from side to side, encouraging the batter to flow left and right, to flood (not too deeply) the hot (but not too hot) metal with batter. It is about gauging exactly how much batter to use (too thin and you have a moth-eaten cake, too much and you have a duvet).

There is a moment, often on Pancake Day, though other days will work too, when I get into the rhythm of it all. It is often about four pancakes in when the mixture, pan, eye and wrist work in well-oiled unison. Flushed with the success of three passable crêpes, thin and lacy and almost too beautiful to fill or dust with sugar, I feel I could keep going all day, turning out perfect pancakes, one after the other. The euphoria is often brief, when I start to get sloppy and overconfident, the pan gets too hot and my work begins to burn.

There is a back and front to a pancake, the most picturesque being the one with a million tiny pockmarks. The back of the pancake is the one that is mostly pale and cooks with scorch marks and blisters. This is the one to go on the inside, the one on which to spread your filling, so when filled or folded the better side, the mottled, honey-hued and lacy side, is facing your critics.

I come across an old photograph on my phone. An iron plate sprinkled with some sort of powder – possibly Parmesan – on which sit a pile of three thick, fluffy-looking pancakes the size of the large buttons you get on a donkey jacket. They are studded with herbs and sprinkled with chives. I long to know where I ate them, and, more crucially, if it was me who made them.

A moment of magic

You are making a chocolate mousse. You have melted the chocolate in a bowl over simmering water and carefully stirred in the butter and the beaten egg yolks. The egg whites are whipped – fluffy, like clouds – and you must now mix the two together.

Another day you are making a cake, the butter and sugar have been beaten to a thick cream, light and soft like ice cream. You have sieved together the flour and baking powder. It is now time to fold the dry ingredients into the wet.

I look forward to these moments, the few seconds, a minute at most, that are crucial to the success of a recipe. There is a little skill involved, the need to combine the two sets of ingredients together thoroughly, evenly, but also – and this is the crux of the matter – gently, so the air is not knocked from the egg whites. The cook must find the balance between being firm and thorough and being light and tender. Mix too thoroughly and you will bash the air from your whites, and your mousse will lose lightness; fold your cake mixture too slowly and the raising agent will start to work even before it gets in the oven. It will shoot its bolt too soon.

As a cook, this is one of those times when I need to be light, gentle, quick, thorough, tender and firm all at once. It is essential to understand that this is when things happen. A moment in the kitchen that is part craft, part alchemy and, it must be said, part magic.

In Osaka, at a tempura counter. The chef lifts little fishes from a tank and drops them into the batter and then instantly into a cauldron of sizzling oil. Seconds later, what arrives on my plate is three little fishes encased in pale, frilly batter, their bodies arched and leaping, frozen in time.

Digging into the undercrust

Many years ago, around the early 1980s, I penned a story about fruit crumble in a rather delightful, now defunct, magazine called *Food Illustrated*. The point of the piece was not so much the crust (to which I suggested adding coarse brown sugar or ground almonds or oats) or the luscious fruit (gooseberries, damsons, rhubarb or plums) that lay sleeping beneath.

The point was to identify what I consider to be the best bit, neither crust nor crumble but the layer of fruit-soaked dough that lies just beneath the crust. It is often a rich purple colour or, in the case of apple crumble, the hue of heather honey. The hidden dough takes on a consistency that is both dry and wet and for which the most accurate description might be plumptious, if that was actually a word. I referred to it then as the undercrust, a term I have watched slowly spread.

The undercrust of a crumble is only one of several such silken treats that await us. The layer of soggy dough where shortcrust pastry meats gravy in a steak or chicken pie for instance. The point at which custard meets sponge in a trifle or, now I come to think of it, that bit of the suet dumpling that sits in the sauce of the stew, richly sodden with flavour and plump with aromatic liquor.

Through the garden gate

Finding primroses

I have missed the school bus again. I am first on in the morning, so need to be up and ready, shoes polished, tie knotted, long before the others. Missing the bus happens once, sometimes twice a week and is not an attempt to get out of maths or soccer practice. Rain, sleet or snow, I have no alternative but to walk.

My route to school takes me along country lanes and mossy hollows, past streams and through woods. It takes me along slippery farm tracks and past cottages with honeysuckle round the door. I notice every detail. No wild rose, hawthorn, apple blossom, spider's web or bird's nest escapes my eagle eye. I know the whereabouts of each cattlegrid, style, cesspit and lover's lane. I also know the whereabouts of the best primroses.

No wild plant is as heart-warming to me as a primrose. No wild daffodil or arum lily, cherry blossom or violet can lift my spirits in the way a clump of primroses does. Their flowers, a soft frosty white like a canary's breast, and their tufts of light-green leaves are dotted under the hedges and hidden deep in the verges. The most beautiful are those I discover growing in the mossy rocks in the lane to the farm, itself covered by a roof of tangled ivy; the flowers twinkle like stars amongst the dark, damp rocks.

We have some at home too, self-seeded, pale-lemon cushions in the rough grass in the orchard. They are the flowers of my childhood.

Kitchen table, spring afternoon. Sorting seeds for the vegetable patch. A glass of fino sherry the colour of straw.

Gardening gear

My favourite jumper – do we not all have one? – has smudges of paint, and my 'smartest' jeans come complete with an olive-oil stain or two. At least, I *think* it is olive oil. The right clothes for the right job is a rule of thumb to which I have aspired but never quite lived up to.

Gardening is a different matter. Step into the border, secateurs in hand, and a random rose will pull any number of threads on your beloved cardigan; water the pots with a hose and your shoes will get soaked and never look the same again. I have scratched, torn and stained countless garments 'just popping out into the garden', so now there is a garden jacket, jumper and shoes that are reserved for anything that involves even the briefest of tasks outdoors.

The jacket is a brown worker's coat that I can throw in the wash once in a blue moon; the jumper a shapeless moss-coloured one that doesn't mind being removed when I get too hot halfway through a job and hang it on a rose bush. The shoes are a pair which, being ever so slightly too big, I can slip on and off in seconds. (Something on which I decided after watching more professional garden workers struggle with soggy laces and shoehorns every time they come in to put the kettle on.)

Am I a better gardener for having 'gardening clothes'? Of course not. But I do feel as if I belong, which is in contrast to donning chef's gear, when I just feel like an imposter (and so I should). That is only part of the story. Gardening clothes smell like the garden. (Mine smell like the potting shed I do not have.) Unlike cooking, which always makes your clothes smell awful, the garden seems to have a thoroughly virtuous effect on whatever clothes you wear. They smell and feel totally comfortable, benign, familiar and with a vague whiff of hard work about them.

February has brought a beautiful melancholy to this garden, as if a soft grey mist has descended. A rectangle of dark-green ivy, black-green yew and walnut-brown beech leaves, the garden, though small and urban, carries a certain peaceful gravitas at this time of year.

Planting narcissi

Petals the colour of butter, primroses and farmhouse Caerphilly. Deep egg yolk and elephant's tusk. Others of piercing marigold, honey and Dutch orange. Trumpets of turmeric, saffron and Sienese alleyways. The narcissi I am planting have petals, coronas and stamens in all the colours of spring. The colours of a child's hand-made Easter card.

The single narcissi are those I cherish most, as much for their scent as their simple, uncluttered form. Many are placed singly in small, chipped terracotta pots. They will sit snugly between larger terracotta pans of Thalia, miniature scented daffodils the colour of buttermilk, and Jetfire with its orange trumpet. There will be a deep pot of Paperwhites and the scrunched creamy-orange Erlicheer. I'm digging in Avalanche with its tangerine fairy cups and Chinese Sacred Lily, which I fear I have acquired for its name alone. My plan is for a zinc table of spring yellows in all the colours of milk on its journey to cheese.

Narcissi, their petals and their scent, carry the spirit of Easter. Planting them on a warm afternoon in November is something of an act of hope. The belief that spring will come once again, and that I will be around to enjoy it. If not, then perhaps someone else will.

Here and there a single rose, usually a tightly pursed bud of the Bengal Crimson amongst the snowdrops and hellebores, like a bloodstain on a dress shirt.

Mr Fox

I am at war with Mr Fox. The most stone-hearted and antisocial visitor to this garden, bringing in bags of other people's rubbish (nappies, anyone?) and scattering them over the flower beds. I can imagine him grinning, teeth shining in the dawn light, as he leaves yet another calling card on my front steps. Those who describe others as being 'as mean as cat shit' have clearly never stepped in that left by a fox.

He wakes me with blood-curdling screams, wrenches the wall-flowers from their pots, deposits the worst imaginable rubbish in the flower beds (the dismembered-doll affair was particularly creepy) and chews the wooden handle of my favourite trowel. He has stolen and shredded several pairs of leather gardening gloves, and I can only assume it was he who dug up and trashed the newly planted hostas.

And yet, catch a glimpse of Mr Fox on a winter's morning, walking leisurely up the garden path at dawn, and you cannot help but stand at the window in awe. The tan, black and white of his fur, as if newly washed and brushed, is splendid enough, but more so his posture, stiff-shouldered and bushy-tailed, and his light-footed confidence, that of a seasoned poacher. I hate him and his habits with a passion, yet always look forward to catching a glimpse of him swaggering up the path, more than a little envious of the way he lords it over the garden. It is clearly he, not I, who owns this space.

The delight of seeing a hand-made hazel hurdle on an allotment.

Pruning the roses*

My father is wearing his gardening cardigan, with its leather buttons and darned elbows. He is holding his secateurs. (Even now it is hard to picture him without his beloved 'snips' in his hand.) They had a blunt, rounded end like a bird's head, a screw where the eye would be, and when open they reminded me of a parrot in flight. He never lost them, unlike his son, who manages to mislay his with frustrating regularity.

He is taking me round the garden, rose bush by rose bush, passing on his pruning wisdom. We snip away any dead branches, then tackle the live ones, cutting on a diagonal to just above the second bud from the bottom of every shoot. He contemplates each incision for several seconds before making an assured, decisive cut. This is a task he clearly relishes, just as he does taking a belt to his son.

I am not keen on the roses in our garden – nor their form, which is one of fat petals that come to a point like an onion. Every one of them is ugly to my eye, but they are the flowers of the 1960s, hybrid tea roses, and 'all the rage'. Along the drive is a particularly hideous arrangement of screaming coral-red (the rose from hell) next to a variety called Blue Moon, a depressing washed-out mauve.

But there, climbing up the whitewashed brick walls of the garage, is the rose of my dreams, a rose so utterly charming, so delicate and fleeting that I can forgive him his screeching reds and

---

* Pruning the roses is the single thing my father ever taught me. Which may explain why the contents of a man's toolbox remains, to this day, a complete mystery. I can't even hammer a nail in without the plaster shattering like icing on a Christmas cake. Still, I can prune a rose, and I thank him for that.

wishy-washy purples. It is rarely without a flower, its petals open wide, in shades of cream, faded fawn and soft pink, and here and there a crimson petal or two. Each summer it is as if a hundred butterflies have come to rest on the wall, baking in the late-afternoon sun. (This rose, *chinensis* Mutabilis, is to this day my favourite.) My father prunes this one with even greater thought, as if each cut is hurting its delicate, wispy stems. The tiny buds, like pink pearls, are smaller than the rest and he ponders each cut like a chess move.

Frost ferns in the corner of a windowpane.

The first spring rain

It is as if everything has overslept. Only the moth-like blossom of the early cherries has emerged, fragile and pale, almost wan. A frail child recovering from illness. The trees and bushes in the garden and parks have been showing buds for a while now, but you need to look closely. The crimson dots on the branches of the roses and azaleas, tight green on the orange blossom and purple on the soot-black twigs of the canadensis. This winter, long, dry, almost interminable, has left the ground parched.

And now, suddenly, the rain. Sweet, steady, gorgeous. You can see the leaves bristling, fronds quivering with happiness. The garden fairies that are the epimediums are dancing. The ground and its plants are suddenly quenched after its long, dry winter. Restored, refreshed and ready to go.

A vase of tulips, whose flowers have faded and whose stems are curling crazily.

Crocuses in the snow

Late February has brought crocuses to cheer us in the melancholy of winter. The petals – white, lilac, mauve and gold – are perfect against a grey-white sky. We planted a thousand small, hairy corms and a couple of hundred have come up. Plucky little flowers, they must fight against the rain, mice, squirrels and sparrows, all of which seem hell-bent on their destruction.

Most welcome are the luminous white Jeanne d'Arc, which have swan-like petals with a tuft of egg-yolk-orange stamens. Others include Orange Monarch, a deep saffron and mauve, and a few Pickwick, the palest lilac with a delicate feathering of mauve. Common varieties, but none the worse for it.

You may not know that some varieties are fragrant too. Rather than needing to crouch on hands and knees to enjoy them, I have plans to plant the bulbs at sniffing height in wide, shallow terracotta pots for the garden table.

Today, our second snowfall of the year. More fine and powdery than the last, as if fairies have dusted icing sugar over the beds and hedges in the night. As the sun starts to shine, the crocuses are at their most beguiling, sitting under the rustling leaves of the beech singing their hearts out in the snow, their throats open in the spring sunshine like hungry fledglings in a nest. This is possibly the genus at its most endearing. You would need a heart of stone not to be enchanted by the sight of a crocus in the snow.

My heart sank when they first appeared, as the flowers were larger and less charming than I had hoped, but then I became grateful for that, as the garden is viewed mostly from indoors at this time of year. The flowers sing against the browns and greys of the February garden, their petals as fine as butterfly's wings and twice as cheerful.

The first blossom seen from a train window.

The wicker baskets

On the stone terrace, either side of the path, are two wicker baskets. As wide as they are deep, they stand guard, their contents changing with the season.

We line them with sacking to stop them leaking soil, which is mostly rotted leaves and organic, sweet-smelling mulch. As I write, the day before New Year, they are covered with a lantern of hazel twigs, tied at the top with tarred string, a precaution against the grey squirrels that dig in search of bulbs to play with.

Soon the green tips of the tulips will peek through their dark earth. Planted deep, so the soil can support their long stems, they take a while to appear, but even now I know there is activity below the surface. I am not sure why they call it the dead of winter.

The tulips are usually in flower in March, a carnival of orange, saffron, rust and purple-black. Once they have gone over, as we gardeners say, their petals brown and frail like antique satin, the bulbs will be lifted and replaced with fully grown foxgloves, whose faded notes of lilac, pink and speckled cream will stand tall till it is time for the dahlias to go in.

The wicker baskets will be here, inviting people down the path, until they rot and no longer hold their colourful trappings, when the garden will return to its natural self, layer after layer of green on green.

Leaf skeletons on dark-brown soil.

Trimming the hedges

Early May and a note in my diary reminds me to trim the hedges. My childhood was full of hedges, the tight corset of green privet that ran the entire boundary of the house, orchard and garden; those I passed on the long walk to school, hedges of hawthorn and holly, sloe, blackberry and wild rose. In spring they were a tangle of white froth and carried primroses and cowslips at their base, violets and the odd bluebell that had strayed from the woods. In winter they would be peppered with scarlet, black and rust berries, grey clouds of old man's beard and dew-speckled spiders' webs that hung like diamond necklaces in the early-morning light.

Thirty years on, and with a garden of my own, I planted hedges almost before anything else. Dark-leaved, slow-growing yew to form the bones of the garden; crisp, round-leaved box to frame the fruit and vegetable beds and softer, brighter hornbeam to bring light and movement to the garden. (If ever I had to start again, I would put in mixed hedges, with hawthorn and wild rose.)

All of the hedges require a twice-yearly clipping to keep them strong and compact – stocky as a bulldog – a job I leave to Katie, who helps me in the garden and is more adept with a hedge trimmer than I could ever be. She keeps them straight by eye rather than with the length of garden twine my father used.

Today the box hedges are being trimmed. The yew looks down benignly as Katie pulls the tatty box bushes back into shape. (The yew gets just one trim a year, in late March.) The air is spicy with the scent of snipped leaves. One by one the lines of the garden beds become clear and sharp, neat green frames once again reign in the chaos of the fruit and vegetables that lie within. Each square frame of *Buxus* holds a spilling shopping bag of runner beans on frames, peas, broad beans and nasturtiums that cascade over the edges. Their surface is like green velvet, cut smooth and flat, their sides straight. Rarely has the garden looked so smart.

The trimming is done in May and again, lightly, in August. Even in this tiny urban space, the trimming makes a lot of mess. To stop the twigs and leaves spreading all over the garden we lay large tarpaulins on the paths, otherwise we would be collecting it all for weeks afterwards. The box hedging is what keeps this garden from becoming a shambles – like a strict teacher with a class of naughty, playful children.

The next morning, at dawn, I wake up and look out of the window to the sight of a pair of fox cubs using the perfect, flat tops of the hedges as bouncy castles. I come down to find huge holes in them, deep hollows with broken twigs and calling cards of tufts of ginger hair.

Kyoto; I stop at a tiny restaurant I want to eat at but it is closed. Outside the locked door is a narrow table with a tin bath filled with flowering lily of the valley and a basin of wild strawberries, ripe and begging to be eaten.

Autumn leaves

The garden has rarely looked more beautiful. It has the bones of an old garden – tall yew hedges, ivy-covered walls, clipped topiary – yet is a relative puppy in comparison to the house. The leaves of the medlar are yellow like a ripe pear, the hornbeam gold as gorse, the clipped beeches are crisping to tobacco-brown.

Amongst the ochre leaves are roses: deep-crimson Gabriel Oak, apricot-blushed Lady Emma Hamilton and the final breath of the haunting white Direktör Benschop, which clambers through the yew hedges. There are Japanese anemones – windflowers – and at the far end of the garden, at the foot of the crab apple tree, a cluster of pale-pink autumn cyclamen.

The back of the house is covered by a *Wisteria sinensis* whose long, yellowing bracts are falling now. Sticking in brush and rake, they are the most annoying to clear up. The York stone terrace is hidden under piles of vast golden fig leaves, curling like grasping hands. As the autumn nights creep in I watch every leaf coming to the end of its life, the garden slowly closing its eyes and falling into a golden slumber.

A cardboard box of persimmons, glowing deep pinky-orange like fat, round candles.

Moss

There is nothing softer on which to walk. Your footsteps are silent, as if treading on velvet; each step becomes slower and more cautious. To set foot on a moss path, even the short one at the top of my garden, slows your pace, every movement now more thoughtful.

The luminosity of moss is extraordinary. It holds water, a dampness reminiscent of cloisters and cathedral walls. I imagine that is how the walls of a monastery might smell.

There is a rectangle of moss in my garden, the roots embedded in small, red bricks. They have an open texture that I suspect makes them hold the water the roots need to live.

As with cats, you can't tell moss what to do. It will survive or not as it wishes. You can provide it with what you feel is the right location and atmosphere, but it may simply refuse to accept your hospitality. Moss is a law unto itself. I curse those who take a power-washer to their stone and brick, rinsing away any hope of softening the surface with even the thinnest film of green.

You can buy it in sheets to get started on a moss garden of your own and place it where you hope it will be happy. You can only cross your fingers and pray. There is always the possibility that it will like the home you have made for it.

Moss looks for places that are damp rather than wet, shady (it is unlikely to survive in full sun) and with clear air – as with lichen, it dislikes pollution. It grows best on the compacted clay soil of which my garden has plenty. The golden rule is never to let it dry out. Once established, you can encourage it with water and a light application of seaweed fertiliser.

There are many who rake the moss out of their lawn. I have a special broom for mine, a fine, short-handled besom that brushes the leaves from the moss without damaging the soft tufts in the way a stiffer-bristle broom might. I tend to leave the petals from the nearby Mutabilis rose. The rose, pink, magenta and fawn-coloured petals scatter themselves quietly over the green suede.

I irrigate the moss in my garden using a watering can fitted with a fine rose. Few sights are more calming than watching fine rain fall on a carpet of moss. Should I forget to water, especially during the winter months, the moss forgives me and bounces back after a soaking. I can't imagine moss holding a grudge.

My ashes would be happy in any of the moss gardens I have visited in Japan. They would like the hush that accompanies these deep-green spaces. Loud voices seem at odds in such a garden. I imagine one always whispers in the presence of moss, as one might when observing a piece of fine porcelain or a religious relic. I would at last rid myself of those who speak in raised voices.

The bushes with the wooden hats

Kyushu, late January. You cross the little stone bridge in your noisy wooden geta. Bow to miss a low-hanging branch of the cedar tree, then stop and breathe in deeply. The watery scent of moss, wet pine needles and cold earth is sweet and you take it in, slowly, as enriching as soup.

Each low, clipped bush – azaleas and box – is shaped like a large cobblestone and has a perplexing wooden canopy, like a little kennel. Protection from the foxes, perhaps, and to stop people sitting on them?

It has snowed in the night and I realise their purpose, their reason for being. When the snow is heavy, which it can so often be, the weight of it can snap the delicate branches of the bushes that are now as old and brittle as a brandy snap. Each plant hides in the shadows, its branches protected, next year's buds safe from frost, cosy under its wooden canopy.

They look after the elderly here.

Nature reclaims the garden

The branches of Souvenir de Madame Léonie Viennot, the old French rose that climbs up the kitchen wall, are tangling with those of the black fig, which long ago became entwined with the wisteria. The pots of carnival-coloured dahlias have outgrown their woven hazel frames and lie collapsed on the terrace like exhausted revellers at Glastonbury.

Late September, and the back garden is at its most wild and, to my eye, its most entrancing. A wine-red rose has climbed into the medlar tree and a single-petalled white one is mounting the tall yew hedges. The wisteria is at its fullest, the leaves starting to turn gold in the autumn light. The zinc top of the garden table is strewn with the fallen petals of pelargoniums that are, in early autumn, outgrowing their pots.

The green borders – mostly ferns, hydrangeas and yew balls – are dotted with white Japanese anemones that sway, true to their common name of windflowers, in the breeze, and the paths are a mixture of gravel and faded, fallen leaves. It feels as if nature is reclaiming the garden, which only a few weeks ago was as crisp as a freshly laundered shirt. A green garden clipped and preened and trimmed to within an inch of its life.

To enter the middle garden through its tall iron gate you must now duck under a *Cercis canadensis*, whose heart-shaped leaves are the colour of fruit gums, and dodge the trailing potentillas that spill from the deep verdigris copper. Viburnums will brush your ankles, spiders' webs will tickle your face and you will return to the kitchen with leaves in your hair. Nature wants you back as well as the garden.

A magical garden in Amsterdam

We drive a little way from the city to a courtyard full of long tables, where we are celebrating the publication of *The Kitchen Diaries*. We sit under a pergola entwined with vines and fairy lights in the warm September air.

The garden, more of an allotment really, is ink-black now, its path illuminated by hanging lanterns on tall, crooked sticks. Rust and saffron sunflowers tower above us, lace umbrellas of fennel and pots of scented pelargoniums glow in the dim light. Bunches of dahlias – yellow, burgundy and fuchsia-pink – sit in jam jars on low tables along the hoggin path. Wild roses grow in tin buckets. Moths flutter in the shadows and everywhere the rich, heavy perfume of night-scented stocks.

This is a garden as if drawn by seven-year-old me. Single hollyhocks and gangly sunflowers tower above a winding, well-worn fence of split hazel. Poppy seed heads rustle in the breeze, rickety gates are propped open by enamel buckets that someone has filled with gladioli. This is tended space, but one where nature is also being allowed to run its course. Either way, there is magic at work here.

I get far more pleasure from arranging objects on a shelf than I probably should. Give me a group of bowls, a jug and a tall pot and I'll give you my attempt at a Morandi.

Pruning the trees

Pruning the greengage tree in stinging rain. I drag a splendid bough into the house, its branches stippled with breaking buds and green lichen, and wriggle it into a basket of logs by the fireside. I have little hope of the blossom opening.

Two weeks later and the blossom has opened, the white petals as delicate as snowflakes, the twigs speckled with small flowers that smell like talcum powder. No vase of flowers or potted plant, no objet d'art or painting can compete with the sight of a branch of single white blossom arching across a room.

Pruning has always been a job to relish. I saw the branches by hand, with a serrated blade that I fear is no sharper than it should be. My journey started with roses but now I will prune anything that doesn't involve climbing. Two trees in the garden receive the most attention from my pruning knife: the fig and the medlar. Both have vigorous limbs that repair themselves in a matter of weeks.

I follow the traditional pruning season, cutting only when the trees and bushes are dormant, which means that most of the work is done on dry, cold days. I wear brown leather gardening gloves as I am careless, even with a blade in my hand. Any handsome branch will be brought into the house, with or without blossom, to fill the rooms with the smell of cut wood and moss, a simple act which makes me feel less guilty about taking a knife to something that is still living.

Wrapping a tree

The ice in Seoul has not melted for days. Scarlet berries pepper the hedges. The icy pavements are so slippery I am tempted to walk with one hand on the railings.

In the park there is a circle of bare trees in the snow, their trunks carefully padded with thick straw, bound every few inches with string. Their branches are meticulously wrapped in thick hessian bandages to protect them from the cold. Their arms held aloft, they resemble a group of slim, naked people dancing the hokey-cokey.

Later I find a whole street of wrapped trees, this time in coloured wool, each one different, the patterns vibrant, every tree togged up in mittens and scarfs, and it makes me smile. My guess is that the trees need protection against the harsh Korean winter. Or could it just be that the local residents love them so much they feel the need to wrap them like some owners of small dogs wrap their pooches?

A painting I should dearly like to own is *Nocturne in Black and Gold, The Falling Rocket* painted in 1875 by James Abbott McNeill Whistler. I am unlikely to venture to Detroit, where the picture lives in the Detroit Institute of Arts.

On the roof

I have always looked up. You could measure my life in gables and garrets, gutters and gargoyles. I enjoy spotting a good downpipe (matt-black cast iron, please) as much as I do a much-trodden York stone floor. What lies above head height is often more interesting than that below, especially in cities, where roof tiles and spires are made to be seen by those who live or work up high. The downside is that I often trip, but everything has its pitfalls. Once, walking through London's West End and staring up at the roof terraces, I tripped and fell so badly I ended up in A&E.

I find it particularly pleasing to spot a good roof terrace, especially one endowed with cascading plants. It is the main reason I have always wanted to go to Singapore. There are some rather pleasing examples in Beirut and Paris too, where grey flat roofs have been transformed into magical hanging gardens.

I had lived in this house for a decade or more before I noticed the flat roof, the expanse of grey asphalt that sat on top of the ground-floor kitchen. Despite passing it several times a day through the window on the stairs, I had never considered its possibilities. Once its inevitable leaks had been repaired and the entire roof rendered waterproof, I set about turning it into a garden of sorts.

Few projects have given me more pleasure than spinning a sad, empty roof space into a garden. Access isn't straightforward – you must clamber through a tiny loo window to get out (I have found myself stuck more than once) – and every plant has to be squeezed through the narrow hole and then repotted to give it room to grow.

And those pots must be plastic, as terracotta is too heavy. Luckily, the offending pots are hidden by the parapet wall.

It took several attempts to find plants that could cope with the aspect, a south-facing wall that is both buffeted by the winds and bakes in the summer. After a few mishaps we have settled on acers, azaleas and short conifers. A mixture that looks unintentionally Japanese. Katie is better with heights than me and has installed a trellis for a wisteria that was looking for room to spread. A hydroponic watering system is up there for the summer droughts.

What I hadn't considered was the effect the blazing heat would have on the acers. For a few weeks in early autumn, the leaves of the *Acer palmatum* and the azaleas are simply gorgeous, a display of earthy pink and rust, orange and blood-red, as vibrant as a spice shop in a bazaar.

The luminous green moss that grows on the sides of a terracotta flowerpot.

Settling my spirits

The middle garden is a sheltered space between two tall yew hedges. Measuring just four metres square, it is shaded by a forty-foot *Robinia* Frisia whose canopy gives shadow, and in autumn golden, filtered light.

Planted with Japanese maples, *Daphne odora* and viburnums, I like to think of this part of the garden as 'my little wood'. A path runs through the middle and at its heart is a rectangular patch of old red half-bricks rescued from the cellars of St Pancras, or so I was led to believe by the gentleman who sold them to me for cash. The bricks are covered with a layer of emerald-green moss, thick like a blanket, and an old verdigris copper that spills with ferns and long trails of maidenhair vine.

It is early summer and the viburnums are in flower – white lace parasols that light the gravel path through to the back of the garden. The scent of the mock orange is trapped between the hedges, its lime-green leaves shining bright against the black-green of the yew. There is something secret about this hidden space, one of the few parts of the garden where you are out of sight from the rest of the terrace. No one can see me sniffing the daphne on a winter's morning, on my hands and knees looking at a yellow crocus, or today picking a bunch of single roses that will rest in a jam jar on the kitchen table.

At night the space is filled with the scent of daphne, philadelphus and *Choisya ternata*. Protected by walls and hedges, the leaves still rustle in the breeze, whispering to one another or, perhaps, to me. I fancy this part is occupied by relatives of the *kami*, the sacred spirits of the Japanese forest, which can take the form of trees, of which the *Cornus* Gloria Birkett is now the most splendid, its pale bracts like a shimmer of creamy-white butterflies come to rest.

This is what I had in mind when I planned this garden, a term that some might begrudge for a space that is filled with small trees and an underplanting of moss. But this is a garden to me, albeit no bigger than a picnic rug. 'What are you going to do with this bit?' is a line I have heard more than once from those who don't understand the spirits held in trees and their shadows.

The snow is falling

It is, at last, snowing. It is falling in the back garden, softly covering the table with its low terracotta dishes of narcissi and scilla and the pots of wallflowers, already budding up in droplets of blood-red. It is falling on the high hedges and the crisp brown beehives of beech that stand either side of the path like guards in bearskins.

An hour later and the flakes sit in thick lines on the twigs of the medlar tree and the crossbars of the gates that stand at either end of the middle garden. The paths and stone flags and terrace steps are invisible now, their patches of lichen hidden under the drifts of white. The pots on the table are mere lumps, unidentifiable from the lanterns and watering cans that stand smothered in snow. I look hopefully at the sky for more.

The sunken courtyard

An old zinc-topped table with cedar legs, a floor of worn red half-bricks, terracotta pots of ferns and ivy, tendrils of jasmine climbing the walls. The little basement courtyard outside the kitchen has a microclimate in which the plumage of tree ferns overwinters without protection and pelargoniums are safe from frost. In summer I step out here for my morning coffee, looking up at the cascading pink and apricot rose that covers the kitchen wall. Three or four weeks of softly falling petals.

This space was originally where the builders dumped their rubble, and then became a resting place for dead and dying plants – 'the hospice' – but long before that this was a place of industry. The legend of a bricked-up cellar is etched on one wall, fading paint on another shows the outline of a long-demolished shed. The little kitchen that overlooks the space was once a laundry room with an open fire, one of the few fireplaces in the house that has been bricked up, though long before my tenure.

Once the builders had moved out with their bags and tools I set about making a little courtyard of the space, though that is a grand word for what is essentially a two-metre-square basement. We found the bricks, sweet little things as thin as crispbread and no longer than an index finger, and laid them over the floor. Katie strung steel cables from one wall to another on which to trail jasmine, roses and fairy lights. We filled zinc planters with maidenhair vine and planted a climbing white hydrangea to wind its way up the rusting iron balustrade.

I set pots of pink pelargoniums and ivy on the little flight of stone steps that climb to the main terrace and covered the table in potted ferns. Most of the nearby properties have taken this space inside the house as part of an extension, but I resisted. This little garden is a sanctuary, a secret, hidden place.

The felling of the horse chestnut

There were fifteen of them. Trunks too wide to hug, standing proud and protective, shielding the terrace from the main road and its traffic. In late spring each horse chestnut was lit with cream candles, a row of frothing soda fountains. Under their vast canopies lay years of the gardeners' gold that is well-aged leaf mould, a few narcissi in spring and the occasional elder tree.

Mine was the first to go. The death knell was sounded by an insurance company, who insisted that the tree's roots were burrowing under the house. We fought and lost, and the tree came down. Locals stood and watched in tears as the grandest of them all, the one outside my house, was removed and its vast wooden corpse carted away. The house, hidden for two centuries behind the chestnut leaves, lay exposed, the first-floor drawing room now visible to each passing bus. We felt naked.

Two weeks later the tree's replacement, a spindly, fern-leaved honey locust, arrived and was planted without much ceremony other than a good watering-in by me. The variety was apparently chosen for its successful survival rate in challenging urban conditions and for its compact root ball. I liked it immediately for its delicate pinnate leaves that carry the same lightness as the robinia in the back garden, and later for its golden autumn foliage. I agreed to take care of it in its early years, trudging back and forth with the hosepipe. It has yet to display the points of cream blossom that appear in spring and I look forward to tasting the sweet paste from its pods that give the honey locust its name.

A few months later, two neighbouring horse chestnuts fell in a storm, crushing cars and trapping residents inside their homes till they could be lifted. Then others were removed at the hands of the local council, wary that they, too, might fall. Their remains are still present, stacked untidily on the green verge, making homes for beetles and bees and perhaps even a hedgehog. The local squirrels play amongst their limbs, hiding nuts and stashing my carefully planted crocus bulbs.

If the death of the horse chestnuts brought sadness, the extra light their felling provided brought unexpected joy. Just as sunshine fills the house from the west, it now does from the east too. Each morning, the rooms to the front flood with early light. The tree's demise has also opened up the green space beneath, allowing spring primroses and apricot-coloured epimediums to thrive.

And another joy ... the small Japanese cherry tree that had struggled in the shade of the chestnut has now found its feet. In a heartbeat it has put on girth and height, a sudden spurt of growth as if in a hurry to fill the vacant space and cover our nakedness. For three weeks in May the blossom flutters in the breeze like a million white butterflies, then covers the underlying hawthorn and spiraea bushes with tiny petals. A silver lining of the very best sort.

Arriving at a friend's house with a cake in a box and a bunch of flowers from our own garden.

The softness of foxgloves

Late May and the tulips are being replaced by foxgloves. Their spires of marshmallow-pink, apricot and maroon freckles on cream throats make them easy plants to love. Unashamedly old-school, they tap into the same seam of garden romanticism as lupins, delphiniums, wallflowers and hollyhocks. They never seed naturally in my garden so they must enter as fully grown plants, thick-stemmed and heavy with buds. I never begrudge the not-inconsiderable price charged. After all, someone has had to nurture them for a year or two.

Planted today, the lower buds already open, it is extraordinary to see how quickly their violet and cream spikes soften the garden's straight edges. Some go in the deep terracotta pots, others are installed in the green beds amongst the topiary, introducing a curiously *Through the Looking-Glass* note to the garden.

The perfume of wallflowers

Clipped topiary, yew hedges, ferns and moss are the base notes of this garden, there when the spring bulbs have gone back to sleep and the blossom has fallen. Like old friends whose presence is unshakeable, they are with me through thick and thin.

The roses are very much the heart notes of the space, spilling from the formal green architecture in shades of apricot, white, buff and deep, arterial crimson. They bring a classical beauty and a certain untidiness, something this garden needs if it isn't to look uptight, and layers of fragrance and softness to a design made up of crisp greens.

The top notes, fleeting, like butterflies, are grown in terracotta pots that change with the seasons. Narcissi, tulips, foxgloves and dahlias. The most fragrant of the top notes are the tubs of rust and maroon wallflowers whose sweet scent wafts on the breeze from February to April. They watch over the garden's annual transformation from brown to piercing acid-green.

The colours of the Persian Carpet variety are those of an old, faded photograph. Should I be asked, 'What is the smell of your childhood?', my answer would undoubtedly be 'Wallflowers'. Looking through old photograph albums, it is that smell – there is a touch of Parma Violets about it – that wafts up from the pages.

The plants are at their best as they first start to go over, short brown stems on which a thousand moths have come to rest. Their scent persists even when the colour has drained from their petals. For many years I picked up wallflowers as my parents had done, by the thick bunch from the greengrocer's, where they were sold in apple crates, their roots coated in sand and cheap as chips. This year I chose deep-red and rust varieties, colours I felt would be in harmony with the orange tulips and saffron trumpets of the miniature narcissi I planned to plant amongst them. But they have failed. Tiny flowers on stunted stems, their petals yellow instead of the promised red and rust and, to add insult to injury, they have no discernible perfume. For the first time in as long as I can remember, my spring garden is without a single wallflower.

You are gardening and it starts to rain but you are having such a good time you just carry on regardless.

The garden fairies

There is, after twenty years, a weight and permanence to the garden. Though small, the walls and hedges, paths and trees have given the space a certain gravitas. This is especially noticeable in the 'middle' garden, with its heavyweight woodlanders, the viburnums and hydrangeas, edgeworthia and acers. An underplanting of hellebores and snowdrops has successfully lifted the solidity, but what I really want is something to give an airy note, a lightness of planting, something ethereal and floating. What I often refer to as fairy dust.

The best of these has been the *Anemonopsis macrophylla*, tiny lilac flowers hanging down from black stems as thin as spiders' legs. Dancing in the breeze, they soften the planting and are particularly magical at dusk when their flowers seem to glow in the fading light. They carry the sort of petals you could imagine one of Cicely Mary Barker's Flower Fairies wearing.

Everyone needs fairies at the bottom of their garden.

Filling the copper

Halfway up the garden, between the yew hedges and the tall iron gates, is a copper. Originally used for boiling vast amounts of water for laundry, one has come to rest in my garden. Filled with a recipe of potting compost, leaf mould and garden soil, it has sat on a patch of mossy bricks for several years now, its sides green with verdigris, plants tumbling over the rim. The copper lies at the heart of the middle garden.

In my old notebooks are lists of plants that have graced this capacious planter over the years, from a giant and hideously expensive mountain pine that failed despite having the correct soil, partial shade and not too much water to last year's spectacle of Black Parrot tulips and burnt-orange wallflowers. The pots and planters here serve a purpose – with so much of the garden staying the same, I need the occasional space in which to have a bit of fun.

I have this year's notebook open, the heading 'Copper 2023' written in blue-black ink, but then the page goes blank. This is almost the best part of my gardening year, the planning, the almost whimsical choice of what-will-go-into-the-planter. The opportunities are virtually endless. I write the words maidenhair vine to get the ball rolling, the trailing, round-leaved creeper that is such a signature plant of this garden. Every other addition will need to sit comfortably with long, straggling stems. Pelargoniums spring to mind – they were a huge success last summer – but I would rather not repeat the picture.

I prowl my bookshelves, picking out garden tomes at random, dismissing much but noting some plants as 'possibles' and marking their place with an old Christmas card. This is rather different from choosing climbing roses for a wall or tulips for a pot as the aspect – light shade and sheltered – has to be taken into consideration. The legendary gardener Beth Chatto had a saying, 'Right plant, right place', and it is one of the rules of gardening I have learned (painfully) that it is worth adhering to.

I go with raspberry-pink potentillas.

In Cornwall. A walkway, hollow like a tunnel, through a vast rhododendron. The path is strewn with deep-carmine petals.

Plague comes to the garden

The plague has descended. The fine grey dust and brown leaves of *Cylindrocladium buxicola*, better known as 'box blight', has arrived in the garden. This second visitation appears more dramatic than the first, the hedges turning brown within days of the first sighting. I brush my hand over one of the affected bushes, dry leaves sprinkle the ground, the twigs desiccate, a puff of dust hovers. There is the mushroomy whiff of mildew.

The last few weeks have been warm and very wet, the perfect climate for the blight that is currently ripping through this section of the country. The first attack in this garden was a couple of years ago and all but a couple of plants survived, the majority growing back stronger, but this is different. Each day I wake to find that a whole new section of hedges has succumbed. The garden is being ravaged.

I mention this on social media and am greeted with a chorus of people telling me to get rid of the hedges. It is only my stubbornness that is stopping me.

Midsummer 2013 and my garden is looking more wild and colourful than it has ever done. Beds of annuals in clashing colours, single orange marigolds, deep-purple-pink cosmos, lilac and pink candytuft and sky-blue nigella. The colours all held together by white parasols of *Ammi majus*.

The scented table

High summer, and the long, zinc-topped table is strewn with papers, notebook, laptop and secateurs. There is water, of course, the novel I am reading and a wooden tray scattered with the remains of lunch (the rind of a piece of melon, a speck of San Daniele, a smudge of burrata and a peach stone). There is also a collection of pelargoniums.

The latter are embedded in old terracotta pots, their stems sporting flowers in various degrees of pink from coconut-ice to deepest pomegranate. Their compost is dry to the touch in response to the fate of my previous plants, which died at my hand through my tendency to overwater. Their petals are as delicate as antique lace but I grow them for their leaves, which are scented – lemon, camphor and rose.

There is Edna Popperwell's Ashby, whose leaves smell not of the advertised rose but (to this nose at least) of frankincense. Attar of Roses has furry leaves which remind me of Turkish delight, Orsett smells of balsam whilst Prince of Orange and Queen of the Lemons speak for themselves, the latter of sherbet lemons rather than the fruit. At the top of the garden is a wayward, rambling Copthorne, whose clusters of marshmallow-pink flowers are entangled amongst the bars of the old iron gate. Others are here not for their scent but for the delicate flowers. The diminutive Shannon sends her frilly parsley leaves and straggle of wandering stems over the table. She has no scent at all, but flowers that resemble salmon-pink stars, which twinkle against the watery-grey zinc of the garden table.

The leaves are nothing to look at but show their magic once you rub them between finger and thumb. I use them for a spritz of inspiration as I write, but I occasionally take them into the kitchen too. If you layer their leaves amongst caster sugar in a jam jar they will infuse the crystals with the essence of lemon, orange or rose. Pick the right leaves and you have delicate, scented sugar with which to crown a summer sponge cake or to infuse in a jug of cream for raspberries. Pick the wrong leaves and you will have sugar that smells of mothballs.

A few of my larger plants sit in the sheltered courtyard all winter, close to the warm air from the Aga outlet, but most of them are brought indoors before the first frosts. (By which I mean once it gets chilly at night; I can't remember the last true frost in this garden.) Once inside, they are pruned to no higher than a few inches, then left on the laundry windowsill till spring. If the soil dries out completely they might get a few drops of water, but you need to take care not to soak them. (During the summer the pots are watered only when the soil becomes dry, so their roots are not constantly wet.)

In spring I give each one a good feed, first with seaweed mixture and then, once the buds appear, tomato food. Once the plants have four sets of leaves, their growing tips are pinched out to encourage more bushy growth and the first buds are removed. I then gradually reintroduce them to living outdoors where they will age gracefully. Each spring a new flush of scented leaves appearing on brown, curling stems. Wise-looking old plants, woody and eccentric, whose charm will nevertheless continue for decades.

The day the hedges went

The short box hedges, thick-set and stocky as a rugby hooker, have survived two attacks of box blight and returned stronger for their ordeal. This month they have succumbed to the box moth caterpillar, an evil little creature that has reduced their emerald-green leaves to brown. This gardener is at his wits' end.

This new horror, moving like the Great Fire throughout the gardens in this part of London, is survivable with treatment; the leaves will grow back. But I have had enough. Watching yet another disease rampaging through the hedges is heart-breaking, but it begs the question of what else may be lying in wait. It is with a heavy heart that I have decided the hedges must go.

The box borders are more than merely decorative: along with beech, yew and ivy they form the bones of this small, urban space. They introduce form, structure and gravitas to what is essentially a young garden.

The garden has loosened its belt, kicked off its shoes. Now that the hedges have been ripped up the space has relaxed. It feels airy and light. My garden can breathe.

Like a bird released from its gilded cage, the space can open its wings – the nasturtiums can tumble across the gravel paths; the roses can fall romantically over one another; the dahlias can stand at ease. It is as if the plants had their lips pursed, waiting to speak, and now they are singing. I miss the crispness of the box hedging, the graphic outline when viewed from the top floor of the house. In truth, what I really miss is the control. But even after twenty-four hours, it is clear that the garden doesn't. Out of its tight corset, both the garden and its owner may never look back.

The first snowdrop opens.

A scent of summer

At a rough guess, the terracotta pot of rosemary has stood outside the kitchen door for fifteen years. The plant, bought from Jekka's Herb Farm, has tolerated being mollycoddled and abandoned as the mood takes me, has fought off two attacks of the beautiful though devastating rosemary beetle and battled on through drought and flood.

In February new needles, as bright and green as young spruce, appear on its brown stems. It is the only herb plant I haven't killed. When I first dug in with the spade, when the space was more allotment than garden, I planted thyme, mint, comfrey and curry plant. Chives and salad burnet snuggled in, tarragon rubbed shoulders with hyssop and myrtle, chocolate mint mingled with pineapple sage and dill towered over rocket. I must have had half a dozen different thymes.

This was before I knew that herbs, those quiet, fragrant, angelic additions to the garden, fight like robins. Comfrey and angelica are downright bullies, mint is a serial trespasser and coriander is a diva. Say boo to basil and he'll faint before your eyes.

I have learned to keep my herbs separate, like naughty children in a classroom. For the last few years all have been grown in pots, planters and troughs. It has turned out to be a wise move. A few, mostly the thymes and red sage, object to being confined by walls of terracotta and have done better in deep lead planters, which are also home to fennel and dill, though not together because they tend to argue. In pots they are also easier to move around to catch the best of the sun – something that is more important for basil than coriander, which may go to seed if it spends too much time in direct sunlight.

Now, in the middle of May, the dahlias have gone into the garden proper, vacating the moss-encrusted table on which they have spent their spring and early summer. This is my chance to bring all the herb pots together in one place. A small meadow of dill and lemon thyme, tarragon and lemon verbena, set amidst Attar of Roses and Prince of Orange pelargoniums. I create a pretty enough landscape that is culinary and medicinal, tucking in pots of marigolds and nasturtiums here and there.

The sun hangs low, a breeze sets in and my work is done. I run my hands through the tallest fronds and gently ruffle the leaves – trails of aniseed and pepper, chocolate and lavender, rose and lemon dance on the breeze. There are hints of cinnamon and curry, camphor and orange, mint and something I can't quite put my finger on. My hands smell of Greek hillsides and Provençal fields, an Elizabethan knot garden and a Parisian apothecary, but they also smell of long lunches in the garden. As I head in to make supper it dawns on me that spring has finally slipped into summer.

Laying the first table of summer in the garden.

The butterfly and the kitchen carpet

I hang a weary, though still beautiful, Bokhara carpet from the kitchen over the garden bench to air. (You can vacuum a Persian rug as much as you like, but nothing removes the dust like a good beating in the fresh air.) As it sits in the sun in shades of faded rust, orange, camel and brown, a butterfly lands. At first bright as a button, the colour of the butterfly's wings seems to fade. The two vivid-orange spots on its forewings quieten to pale ochre; the black outer edges fade to grey; the colours, once so sharp and clear, calmly take on the colours of a moth. The light perhaps? The reflection from the carpet in the butterfly's wings, or simply a way to disguise itself to predators? The butterfly sits there for what seems like an age. Silent, resting, occasionally unfurling its velvet wings, the colours of which are now almost identical to those of the carpet. Hiding in plain sight.

A May morning, summer is finally here. The garden has never looked better.

The scent of a summer evening: 1

By early July the jasmine is back in full feathery leaf, climbing the walls, holding onto the jagged face of the faded red bricks. At night the walls of the sunken garden, the red-brick courtyard, trap the perfume. As you descend the stone staircase the smell wraps itself round you like a cashmere shawl.

Once established, jasmine grows well in this garden, and there are three, no, four varieties now. A soft yellow, like clotted cream, that hangs loosely from the window boxes, shifting in the breeze. A pink variety, *Jasminum stephanense*, clambers up the brittle, naked stems of a much older plant, using its relative as a trellis. White stars of *Jasminum grandiflorum* cover the tendrils that have woven a canopy over the courtyard, a fragrant white parasol whose petals fall like snowflakes each autumn.

Then there are the pair of *Trachelospermum jasminoides*, unrelated to the jasmine family but with such a similar flower and scent one could be forgiven for assuming they are sisters. This variety wears shiny, holly-green foliage and has twisted, snow-white flowers. Often known as Chinese jasmine, two of them cover the boards at the bottom of the garden.

It is late evening, the scent is rolling through the garden even without a hint of a breeze. A faint, ghostly presence at first, light and soft as soap, as if someone has walked past leaving perfume in their wake. Now, in what remains of the day's heat, the scent starts to engulf, swirling around me. I can taste it in my evening drink. By the time night has fallen the smell is almost hallucinatory; my temples are aching.

Some plants give out their strongest scents during daylight, attracting bees and butterflies; like phlox and many lilies, jasmine keeps its headiest moments for the night, to attract moths, which are the plant's most efficient pollinator. Before I go to bed, I once more walk around the garden, grabbing handfuls of scented air and cupping my hands to my nose.

The scent of a summer evening: 2

It is too dark to read, but light enough to stand barefoot on the stone terrace, drink in hand. The end to one of those sultry summer days when nary a leaf has moved since dawn and the bees bump their way around the garden, stoned on heat and nectar. The butterflies move so slowly you could catch them in your hand.

The air is heavy, almost oppressively so, with the scent of jasmine and roses. The high hedges of this garden trap the scents of daphne and narcissus in winter and rose, honeysuckle and jasmine in summer, which was always my intention. This method of holding fragrance between the small 'rooms' of the garden is one of the few matters in which I might have succeeded. I long to grow madonna lilies or evening primrose, night-scented stocks or lavender for their fragrance alone, but tonight it is the turn of the climbing white jasmine to engulf us. The heat of the day may have been calmed by the sun's setting, but it is still held by the stone terrace and old walls of the kitchen. Tiny moths are now out in force, flitting amongst the tangle of jasmine stems.

The roses were originally picked as much for their perfume as for their colour and form. (Unlike my first roses, which were bought purely because I was enchanted by their romantic names.) Of the basic musk, myrrh, tea, fruit and old-rose fragrances I am drawn to the latter two. Fruity is a broad brush on a night like tonight. Lady Emma Hamilton, reliable though now retired by the growers, is at her most giving: apricots and white peaches spring to mind. Gertrude Jekyll is one of the most intense of the old-rose scented varieties. She calls me over every time I set foot on the terrace.

Unlike the more generous jasmine, even the most scented rose requires us to bend a little, pushing the tip of our nose into the cluster of petals. Not so Gertrude tonight, mingling as she does with the white jasmine, hovering cloud-like over the hot stones of the terrace. I have a plan to bring the Queen of Denmark into the garden too, another old-rose scent, and I long for a decent musk rose such as Buff Beauty, exuding its faint note of cloves on a warm evening.

A neighbour's cat wanders through the garden, his steps slow and thoughtful. He seems particularly contemplative tonight, at one point stopping to breathe in the magical air. A late-evening stroll around what he feels is his territory. We have had 'words' about this but he always wins. I'm a pushover when it comes to felines.

I light candles in the iron lanterns. Dark now, and the perfume seems even more intoxicating under the stars. I move inside and sit in the study. Notes of jasmine and rose are drifting in through the open window, a benign and heady spirit but one that is now starting to make my head swim.

I have climbed over the iron railings of a private garden in London. One of those squares where only the local residents hold the key, most of whom clearly live abroad. I sit on a wooden bench and listen to the garden's nocturnal rustlings and the double delight of snow-white blossom against a dark sky and the delicious tingle of being somewhere I shouldn't.

The Discovery apple

As soon as I moved into the house, I planted a Discovery apple tree at the foot of the garden, by the yew hedge. A gift to the Norse gods for eternal youth, but in truth a nod to the apple tree of my childhood, whose canopy shaded the patch of phlox growing underneath, whose long stems and flowers the colours of sugared almonds hid a treasure trove of fallen fruit.

Discovery is a scented apple, with bright, acid flesh that does not keep well. The small, slightly flattened fruit are best eaten straight from the tree. The flesh is white as frost, flashed lightly with strawberry pink. A child's apple.

It is aptly named. Brought up as I was in a world of Dairylea, Ritz Crackers and Wonderloaf, the flavour and scent of these pale fruits were my first hint that there was something more interesting out there to eat.

My tree, twenty years old now, awaits the lacework of soft-green lichen that covered the branches of my parents' and, infuriatingly, phlox has so far refused to grow beneath its boughs. It is the earliest apple, ripening in August. A fruit I think of not only as the herald of the apple season, with its Michaelmas Reds and Blenheim Oranges, its Cornish Honeypins and Ribston Pippins, but as the beginning of everything.

The desire for a garden shed. Small, with a wooden door and ivy climbing up and over the wooden tiled roof. A pale-yellow climbing rose, *banksiae* Lutea, on one side, an iron boot scraper on the other. There would be room for my garden spade and fork, my boots, a bag of potting compost and a diminutive window so I may over-winter my old pelargoniums in their chipped terracotta pots. It will never happen, but it is always good to daydream.

The greengage tree

Late August and the garden is tired, the air heavy and still. The greengages are ripe, hanging like Christmas baubles from brittle branches, bent double from the weight of their harvest. The fruits, chartreuse, soft as jelly, are the size of a blackbird's egg. They glow as if a candle is burning inside them. I try to pick them before this stage, whilst they still have a bloom, before the birds get to them.

I never planted this tree. It owes its place to my habit of hurling fruit stones into the garden rather than the bin or to the 'butterfingers' of a passing crow. Its blossom is the only sort I bring into the house. An eight-foot bough of it once sat in a tall glass jar in my study for three weeks or more. First in tight rose-pink buds, then a fortnight of pearlescent petals before they fell sleepily to the floorboards.

The fruits are overripe now and taste of wine and honey, but will make the mother of all frangipane tarts. We will gorge on those that are left, let the flesh dissolve on our tongue, then suck at their stones, tossing them back into the garden in hope.

Throwing the latest gardening catalogues in the recycling bin and whispering, 'No, thanks' ... I have enough.

Dog days and jam-jar puddings

We have dragged the dusty carpets onto the stone terrace, their faded colours blinking in the bright sunlight. Cushions too, lumpy with age, much of their stuffing gone, but comfortable nevertheless. We lie on the ground, propping ourselves on our elbows, shaded from the vivid sunshine by the canopy of the fig tree.

There is wine, the pink sort we might drink only on days such as this, and plates of burrata and tomatoes, sliced thickly. I have thrown nasturtium leaves and petals over the tomatoes, their pepperiness akin to basil. The garden, small though it is, is full of lazy bees supping hopefully at the foxgloves – going over now – and the pots of pinks scattered down the length of the garden table.

The stone terrace is barely four paces deep and the width of a terraced house. The flags bake in the sun. This is where I grow pots of tomatoes, Marmande and Gardener's Delight, and Cedric Morris sweet peas, fluttering butterflies of pink cosmos and bright-orange marigolds. There is basil and thyme, lavender and sweet rocket. Here and there are pots of fennel going to seed in the sun. The stones are hot underfoot, the pots beg to be watered almost daily lest the herbs bolt and are the recipients of rainwater from the water butts and salad-washing water from the kitchen, every bowl of which is gifted in their direction. We waste not a drop, nor should we.

The soft pastels and red-wine colours of this garden change in the piercing sun. The deep reds fade to violet and walnut-brown; the pinks, soft oranges and creams crisp like old newspaper. I don't mind, in fact I rather like the faded colours in the glorious heat of late July. I haven't turned the oven on in a week or more. Today burrata, yesterday panzanella and before that rough-and-tumble dinners assembled from the deli. Lunches have been laid out in assorted bowls outside: preserved artichokes in oil, deli-made couscous salads, marinated octopus and tinned sardines. There are lumps of feta scattered with dill and bloomy goat's milk cheeses with rose-petal za'atar.

Pudding is offered in jam jars. Makeshift trifles of sponge, lemon curd and apricots. Messes of meringue, loganberries and cream. Another of passion-fruit posset and halved cherries. In the top of each jar a flower: rose petals on the loganberries, a viola with the apricots, marigold petals scattered over the dark-red cherries. Little pots of treasure in which to go digging with your teaspoon.

Once the sun has gone over the fig tree I can read in its shade. Robert Macfarlane and Roger Deakin; Olivia Laing and Donna Tartt. A delightful dive into Lewis Carroll and revisiting Alan Bennett. Reading a book a second time, as I often do, is like returning to a dish you make time and again. You never tire of either, no matter how familiar they feel.

I have been trying out a few different plants this year. Dahlias the colours of a circus tent, a couple of new golden roses from David Austin and a variety of dark-red nasturtium I haven't grown before. As the garden crisps, it is now I really value the terrace. The residual heat of its slabs of grey stone, the smell of the zinc planters spilling their contents of white rocket and lavender, of dusty sage and creeping thyme. I run my hands through the leaves. The smell reminds me of the south of France. I value the tiny plants that creep through the terrace's cracks, the cushions of purple thyme and tiny white erigeron, like pink-blushed daisies.

What lies beneath the terrace is a mystery. Two arches, long ago bricked up, suggest some sort of cellar. I have resisted exploration.

Sometimes it is better not to know. Whatever is down there, let it rest in peace.

Picking a basket of deep-pink roses for petal jam.

Dreaming of hedges

Lavender would make a fragrant new hedge for the vegetable beds. Spikes of mauve to rub between your fingers as you walked along the path to the end of the garden. 'Step-over' apple trees would provide handsome bones in winter and a snow of pink-flushed white petals in spring. Privet would be green all year, and a partnership of holly and ivy would be dark and sumptuous. There are, however, downsides to each of my daydreams: my rich soil makes lavender feel a little queasy; privet is too pedestrian and unimaginative, like choosing the lamb and the chocolate dessert every time you go out to eat; holly is likely to scratch everyone's ankles and ivy will provide a safe house for snails. The apple option, though delightful, is expensive, way out of this gardener's hedge-fund.

I need to make a decision before the summer sun renders the ground too hard for a spade. I make green tea and take it out onto the kitchen steps; from there I can survey the wide margin of bare soil that now sits round each vegetable and flower bed. I spend a solitary twenty minutes contemplating my dream hedge: a boundary of woven hazel and beech with hawthorn and wild, single roses. I drift off into an imaginary tangle of soft leaves and thorny twigs, the cream-soda froth of white hawthorn and bumblebees getting drunk on dog roses. In autumn there would be glowing haws and crimson rosehips, in winter the rustle of crisp, walnut-brown beech leaves on brittle twigs.

The clock is ticking. An instant hedge feels like one of those makeover garden programmes, fun to watch but lacking any real long-lasting pleasure. I cannot ignore the fact that I am getting

313

older and would like to see the idea come to fruition before I depart. I ponder the garden as it stands, hedge-less, taking in its new soft-ness of structure, watching, spying almost, as plant nudges plant, leaf tickles leaf, branches link.

I finish my tea and come in. Decision made.

A bundle of old newspapers that you start to use in the potting shed, but then get distracted by the stories.

The naked garden

I'm all for nakedness in the garden. The long grey stems of the witch hazel in January, its flowers like fiery orange tassels. The soft buds, downy, like the ears of a rabbit, of a magnolia in March or, most welcome of all, the yellow-white heads of *Edgeworthia chrysantha* – the paper tree – that hang at the end of its branches like bunches of crystallised sweets. There is also, tucked between the yew hedges, the sugar-pink daphne, though it usually keeps a few of its leaves all year, and the *Viburnum × bodnantense* whose clove-like scent you catch as you walk past on a winter's day.

You can try too hard to make a 'year-round' garden, filling it with scarlet dogwoods and salmon-stemmed azaleas, but to do so is to risk overshadowing the occasional surprise that awaits in a less contrived space. Better, I think, to delight in coming across the occasional snowball of pink flowers on a dove-grey viburnum branch on a nippy March morning, or a galaxy of yellow stars amongst the tangled brown stems of a winter jasmine that feels as startling as a shot of lemon juice in your eye.

When I talk of life's small joys, there is no finer example than those few flowers – pollen-dusted catkins and fireworks of witch hazel, furry magnolia buds and marshmallow-pink viburnums – that bring delight to the winter garden.

Walking out into the vegetable patch and always, always finding a stand of rainbow chard, the candy-coloured stems a constant reminder that, yes, I can call myself a gardener.

The tulip diaries

Sweeping leaves from the paths. Job done, I put the kettle on and return to the comfort of armchair gardening. A tulip catalogue, the most hardcore of gardening porn, has arrived. Choosing tulips from the page or scrolling through the varieties on an iPad is one of the greatest treats of the gardening year. It is when I get to wallow in the salacious delights of the crinkle-petalled Black Parrot and Orange Emperor, the brilliant tangerine Cairo that stands head and shoulders above the crowd, or fantasise about the soft ochres of Brown Sugar. The single-flowered, pale pastels are tempting too, if only for their gentleness, their shy colours reminiscent of butter-cream on cupcakes.

The Rembrandts are the tulips of my dreams, great goblets the colour of hot-air balloons; deep plum and crimson with flashes of yellow; tight green and white petals as crisp as ice on a pond and those that look like crushed berries being stirred through whipped cream. These are tulips that truly bring a fever to my online shopping and yet, bizarrely, they remain as dreams, and I once again chicken out in favour of solid colours.

The older I get the more I appreciate the delicate species varieties, brightly coloured fairy cups with spindle stems. More like large crocuses, they carry a charm that the larger versions lack. They are fragile, though, and rarely stand up to my marauding squirrels and neighbourhood cats. I make a list, but looking back in my little brown notebook it hardly varies from year to year. The usual order of glowing-orange lantern shades is joined by a handful of raspberry-pink and white.

November

The bulbs arrive, neatly labelled. I dig out last year's from the cellar, though they rarely come to much. Katie plants them, randomly, deeply, in the hefty terracotta pots that line the short path from the terrace to the garden table. She covers them with a trellis of twigs in an attempt to thwart visiting cats.

February

A cold day, the air as fresh as grated ginger, and I spot the first green tip of a tulip. Days later another, then, as the days pass, the whole surface of the pot is peppered with bright, hopeful shoots. Their appearance hammers home the notion of trusting nature. Buds will open, seeds will sprout, bulbs *will* come up.

Early April

For several years the terracotta pots have been filled with tulips in shades of orange, saffron, rust and apricot. The colour of sunrise and sunset. This year there are splashes of creamy white amongst them to calm the fires of Cairo, Brown Sugar, Orange Emperor and Prinses Irene. The deep-pink ones marry much better than I expected, softening the citrus notes. In fact, I am rather pleased with the effect. Looking out, as I am now, on a garden newly green, the leaves acid-bright against the yew hedges, many a branch is still wearing its brown winter coat – and then I am startled at the uplifting sight of pots of orange tulips, laughing joyously in the spring sunshine.

Late May

My love for the tulip is at its deepest when the flowers start to go over. When the stems curl and twist, the colours fade and the petals become translucent. The stamens are purple-black now and sooty freckles of pollen lie over the table. I delay taking them up to the compost as long as I can, leaving them till almost every petal has crisped and fallen from the stem.

Old roses

The roses are fading. Turmeric petals soften to the colour of old dusters, magenta becomes palest violet, edges that were dark and sumptuous turn to the colour of a tea stain. What was once as white as snow is now buttermilk. Their texture changes too: petals soft and strong enough to support a portly bumblebee dry to walnut-coloured fragments frail and ageing till they shatter.

Digging my spade into the vegetable patch and finding the soil in fine fettle. Dark, light and fecund.

The golden robinia

We cleared the garden, the lawn sliced into squares and neatly stacked, a layer cake of brown turf and green grass. The skinny, leafless fig chopped and ready for the log basket; the wizened stems of purple clematis on the compost heap. The only thing left standing was the *Robinia* Frisia, its trunk split oddly in two, its crown of yellow-green, fern-like leaves about eight metres above us. I debated its removal too, purely because I fancied a blank canvas.

Over the last twenty years the robinia, which is sometimes called a false acacia or black locust, has grown to become a stately resident. She now towers over the garden yet has an airy quality because of her shimmering gold-green leaves and the lightness of her canopy. It is one of three similar trees in the surrounding gardens, though only this is the golden variety, its leaves fizzing like cream soda in late spring, softening to gold as the year moves on. Sometimes, in early summer, the tree's brittle stems are laden with white flowers, like plump wisteria or acacia blossoms, followed by brown seed pods that stay till autumn.

The tree's canopy is light and open, like a lace parasol, and filters the light, sending shimmering shadows over the moss beneath. In the afternoons and early evening the sun hits its golden leaves so the entire tree seems illuminated from beneath. Against the dark greens and surrounding trees it shines on a late summer's evening like a chest full of golden coins.

A few weeks ago, I received the bad news that one of its two trunks must go. The tree surgeon, here to trim the pleached hornbeams that shade the bottom of the garden, has spotted that the wood is rotten and if the trunk should fall it would take a neigh-bour's balconies with it. Seeking planning permission to remove the affected timber feels rather like secretly arranging for a friend to be operated on without their knowledge. Which, of course, is exactly what is happening.

Despite the girth of her trunk and height of the canopy, the robinia carries a certain elegance. She is light on her feet. In some ways, a good tree for a domestic garden. I occasionally daydream about what to replace her with should she succumb to the honey fungus that affects many of her cousins. What tree could ascend to that height yet carry itself with such grace?

Today, she received her surgery.

A piece of driftwood the colour of an old bone, washed smooth by the sea, its surface soft as velvet.

A garden in which to dream

In the grounds of a stately home in the north of the country, chatting with the head gardener who casually drops the subject of fairies into the conversation. Everything about this garden, its antiquity and quiet dignity, a deep sense of spirit and 'good bones', encourages me to go along with his gentle insistence that there are things you leave 'for the fairies'.

If they exist at all, it is here, hidden in the shadows of these time-worn gardens, frolicking amongst the old stones and umbriferous plants, the jiggling ferns, and bathing in the pools of dew that come to rest in the leaves of lady's mantle and hostas.

Some plants grow better in shade. The woodlanders: cream spires of aconitum and aruncus, delicate ferns and the tall windflowers better known as Japanese anemones amongst them. As you might expect, the fairy flowers of thalictrum and epimedium thrive when grown in dappled light and will dance in the gentlest of breezes. The perfect hiding place for those who inhabit the 'otherworld'.

Some humans fare better in shade too. We do not crave the bright lights and the attention it brings but prefer to work quietly, a life lived, if not exactly in the shadows, in a certain cool, dappled light. Always one to dwell more contentedly in woodland than on a sun-drenched beach, I find the half-light with its shadows and needles of bright sunlight a fine place in which to spend my days.

Magnolias, azaleas, Solomon's seal, primroses, violets, dog roses ... all in my list of favourites and all plants whose leaves and blossoms fare best away from harsh light. It is the shadow that provides the definition, but it also offers protection and a sense of serenity.

Those who look after the country's best-known gardens often don't get the recognition they deserve. A few may be shackled by tradition or 'the powers that be', but most seem to balance the history of the garden and its creators with their own creativity. Few gardens stand still, because that is the nature of plants. I just hope that their plans will always leave something for the fairies.

A little more

Finding art

I admire those who find small, beautiful objects by accident: the rusty Georgian iron nail in the gutter; the egg-shaped pebble picked up in the dunes; the eighteenth-century shard of yellow glass from the garden. Small things to treasure.

I have never collected random shells or stones, even when I lived in Cornwall, where I would take a daily afternoon walk along the beach. Shells, I think, are always prettier left in the sand. Stones are pleasing, healing, to touch, something to roll over (and over) in your hand, your fingers sliding over the soft bumps and hollows as if you were stroking a Henry Moore. Those stones have stories to tell, worn smooth by their time in a stream or on a well-trodden path, but again I tend to leave them within the landscape in which they were found.

There are seemingly random collections of stones in the house at Kettle's Yard in Cambridge that I admire, and I have friends who collect them too, making calm arrangements on side tables, desks or window ledges, but it is a craft I have never mastered. I have much to learn.

Driftwood and lichen-covered twigs are another matter. I have always picked up driftwood, its surface worked smooth by the waves. It is the feel of driftwood that appeals, the suede-like patina, like stroking antlers. The colours, like the belly feathers of a sparrow or a rabbit, are gentle. To touch it is to be instantly calmed.

On a walk, it is rare that I fail to pick up a stick, even if that walk is only up the garden path. The branches of the robinia are as brittle as ice. Most days see a lichen-freckled twig fall onto the patch of moss below the tree's canopy. Sometimes I leave them there, other days I will bring the twig in and put it in a small vase. My sort of treasure.

Curds and whey

A moist and milky Lancashire, a Wensleydale with notes of black olives, a magnificently misshapen Blackmount goat's milk cheese, as light and fluffy as snow. Buying British cheese from a specialist is probably the food shopping I look forward to most of all. Bring home a high-baked baguette, its crust crisp and black-etched, and you have me for life.

The smell of the shop is wet and chalky, of milky muslin and yoghurt. As cool as a cloister. The colours are gentle – every shade of white and cream to primrose-yellow – like the first page of an artisan paint company's colour card. The patchy greys and browns of the rinds, the brown of old muslin, the charcoal ash and grey-greens of the mould-speckled goat's cheese are the colours of my kitchen, the shades of lime plaster.

At the sight of a market fruit-and-vegetable stall I feel my pulse quickening, but here, surrounded by the smell of milk in all its stages, my heartbeat slows. This is a place so benign, so calming ... somehow healing.

A black wardrobe full of clothes in different shades of blue. Cobalt and cerulean, woad and indigo, azure and cornflower and the blue-black of the star-speckled night sky.

Dog becomes cat

I was brought up with dogs. First a golden retriever, soft as a brush, solid as a rock, who spent most of his life snoozing by the Aga. Then a thick, terrifying fox terrier (hair like a pan scrubber, bite like a shark) that arrived at my childhood home with my stepmother (hair like a pan scrubber, bite like a shark) and the polar opposite of the much-missed Rak.

For an entire summer, I 'dog-sat' a pair of overenthusiastic springer spaniels. Adorable, mischievous and deeply affectionate, they were quite impossible to exhaust. I would walk for miles through the sand dunes whilst the dogs bounded ahead causing havoc with people's picnics, disturbing nude sunbathers and surprising more than a few lovers going at it in the dunes with a well-placed lick or two. They were also exceptionally successful in finding hideous things in which to roll, a rotting seal being particularly memorable.

I have also shared a home, albeit briefly, with an elderly and rather snooty corgi who once got incredibly drunk at a wedding and a portly, much-loved golden labrador. I was converted to being a cat lover by Norman, a somewhat haughty ginger tom who ruled the roost at a restaurant I worked in during the 1980s. He became something of a local celebrity – even the council's hygiene inspector would ask how he was.

Norman's modus operandi was to target any lone diner, climb onto the seat opposite and stare them out. They would eventually relent and give up a morsel of their dinner to him. He never begged in the way a dog might, his art – and it was an art – was simply to stare, watching every forkful on its journey from plate to lips, silent yet supremely confident that a scrap of cold turkey would be coming his way. A masterclass.

Lichen

If I am to have a tombstone, then I would like it to be made of stone, not granite or marble. I have had a fascination for lichen all my life, and I would rather like to be buried with it, the slow, smoky-green spores growing over my carved N and S, and maybe a little moss on my 'Here lies'. And under a tree, please, for the shade.

I am in Flåm, Norway, and the torrential storm that welcomed us has quelled. We stop the jeep to stretch our legs and have a pee. There is soft ground underfoot, spongy and damp, the river is fast-flowing and I am careful to steer clear of the slippery bank. Lichen is everywhere; even the youngest trees are encrusted with it. Here it is as abundant as I have ever seen it, coating almost every trunk and twig with a soft green crust.

We had smoked salmon for breakfast, with sticky bread like wet peat and cloudberry juice the colour of apricots. A meal so simple and perfect, a breakfast steeped in the spirit of the place. Here in the woods I hear gushing water and birdsong, but little else. Just the crackle of twigs, the occasional drip, drip of raindrops from the trees.

If I could spend the rest of my life here, with the lichen and moss, I would be a happy man.

A glass chandelier, glimpsed through an open window in Venice, its old arms bent out of shape, candles lit, glass droplets in shades of citrine and plum twinkling in the evening light.

Hands on

I climb onto the table, half hoping the lurid rumours are true – the whispers that warn I will be rubbed raw with a metal scrubbing brush, and once the task is finished my new skin will resemble that of a four-year-old. But it is not to be. The masseur is using not a brush but a coarsely woven cloth barely as rough as the wrong side of a crispbread. It may sluff off several layers of dead skin, but I shall not step down from table resembling a scalded pig.

Every massage is different. The technique, the mood, the etiquette. What will it be this time? A naked pummelling like a baker kneading a lump of dough (Hungary) or an hour of whale music with hands that move so tenderly I will be asleep in minutes (Finland)? Will they have fingers like raw sausages (Warsaw) or will it feel as if I am being pecked to death by pigeons (Japan)? What sort of oil will they use? Is this the one that leaves me smelling like cheap bubble bath (Boston) or the one where I end up with a distinct whiff of the balti house? (It once took three days to rid myself of some particularly potent mustard oil applied at a four-handed massage (Thekkady).) Will they scrub me first (Seoul) or dust me with the softest talc afterwards (Vienna)? And will all this take place in a tuberose-scented padded cell (London) or on a wooden bench in a hut with a mud floor (Kerala)?

This is clearly the one I have been waiting for. The therapist scrubs me from head to foot, but not so hard I cry in agony, dries me with a soft cloth, which no one has done since I was six, then starts work with his bare hands and a bottle of jasmine-scented oil. I emerge, if not cherubic, at least half a dozen layers of skin lighter.

The after-effects of massage range from leaving you in deep, nourishing sleep to fizzing like an elderflower cordial. Both of which are a nuisance, and not only to the masseuse. No one wants to pay a hundred quid to miss most of it because they have fallen asleep. (I feel much the same about flying.) Neither do you always get what you went in for. The need for total relaxation that actually left me so wired I couldn't sleep for days (Germany). The energy boost I so desperately needed that rocked me into a coma instead (France).

There are sessions you never want to end (South Korea). Others when you count the seconds (New York). There have been massages in Kerala that involved so much oil, warmed over a night light, you could have wrung me out like a dishcloth. Yet I have had many that involved no oil at all, including one in Budapest where every dry stroke was so painful it was accompanied by the sound of a puppy begging for a walk. There was the bear in Budapest who turned me back to front and inside out; an hour of torture in Berlin when I was scrubbed with what smelled like Daz and brought me out in spots; and a therapist in Marrakech who clambered on top of me and pinned me down like a triumphant wrestler.

I have had massages in almost every country I have ever visited (the exception being Iran). Chances are you will find the massage from heaven when you are thousands of miles from home and will end up chasing that particular dragon for the rest of your life. The one that leaves you floating from the table. But everyone's experience is different. Reviews are notoriously unreliable. Word of mouth is no guarantee either. One person's five-star massage is another's expensive disappointment. And 'firm pressure' can mean anything from being tickled with a feather to being squeezed like you are the last smudge of toothpaste in the tube.

This is the massage to beat all others. Everything about this couple of hours is right. The basic, tiled room devoid of suffocating towels that smell of stale massage oil, drippy 'world' music or cloying scented candles. The rough all-over scrub followed by the firm application of soft, healing oil. The light is neither seductively low nor as bright as an NCP. The only sounds are those of a far-off swimming pool and the churning of a nearby tumble dryer. No frills, no decadence. Just the massage to beat all massages.

Hearing loud opera from a passing car.

Poppy fields

Mum drove a primrose-yellow Volkswagen. It was considered somewhat unusual for women to drive in the late 1950s and even more so to drive fast, but she did both. My mother was gentle, shy and softly spoken, but when she got behind the wheel of her car she drove like a demon. I am surprised I got safely through my childhood.

I am seven or eight and we are driving home from Shifnal hospital, once a workhouse, and home to my maternal grandmother, whose dementia is so bad she needs twenty-four-hour care. We can't have her at home as my great-aunt, also living with dementia, is already residing with us. I guess my parents can't handle a precocious, solitary son *and* two batty old ladies. (I rather think we would make life more interesting.)

I am obsessed with the wild poppies that freckle the cornfield with blotches of scarlet. Innocent, of course, of their links with the dead and the symbolism and poetry with which each flower is indelibly stamped. I am simply fascinated with their silk-like petals, fine, hairy stems and the fact that they grow in the fields of barley and wheat. I implore my mum to stop so I can pick a bunch, and she finally relents. Her reluctance is due partially to the frequency with which I request that she stop the car. She no doubt also has in mind how upset I get when their spindle-stems droop like pieces of string before we can even get them home to a jam jar of water.

The moment you realise the flowers you bought or picked, their stems bent, their faded petals now crisp and brown, look even more beautiful than when you first put them in the vase.

The Raku Museum

A line of jade-green velvet slippers lies in welcome. A quiet but insistent invitation to enter this small museum hidden in the suburbs of Kyoto, smaller than Kettle's Yard in Cambridge or the Louisiana in Copenhagen, yet one that captured my affections more than almost any other.

The tea bowls – for that is what I have come to see – are displayed singularly, in capacious glass cabinets. Each bowl is bathed in low light on a square of purple silk in the middle of a tatami mat. The curation is simple and uncluttered, the lighting is gorgeous, and the bowls – chawans – are breathtaking.

This is the sort of museum in which you talk in a whisper or, better still, hold your tongue. Yet there is much joy here. There is no exhibit that has mesmerised me for longer, where I have spent more time admiring the works, their shapes and shadows and crackled glazes.

One day, I would like one of these bowls to hold my ashes.

At Rachel Whiteread's Holocaust Memorial in the Judenplatz in Vienna. A single votive candle burns silently outside.

The morning fruit plate

Early, the blackbird still silent, the sky charcoal. A flicker of orange light over the East End. The kitchen is cold, but I don't mind that. The cold refreshes. In the long drawer that runs the length of the zinc kitchen counter is a collection of odd, small plates and oval shallow dishes that come out at this time of day. Grey, eau de Nil, pale wintry blue and olive, the colours of early morning. One, a rectangular, dark-green Oribe dish I found in a Sunday-morning flea market, is reserved for fruit. A wedge of loquat-hued melon, a single Russet apple or half a pomegranate that has been cracked open to reveal the cluster of jewels within. In late summer it will support a single, rust-freckled plum; on a late-autumn day a perfect, chubby-bottomed pear.

The plate is a sheet of clay, glazed a shiny, muted green, whose edges turn up as if made to catch the escaping juice of a late-summer peach. There is no fruit which its shape and glaze do not flatter. Two deep-red cherries, joined at the stalk; a glowing, almost translucent persimmon, tender as a bruise; a small bunch of muscat grapes all take on a new significance. Even a standard green-grocer's orange, cut into segments, shines as brightly as a morning star.

Warm fat seeping through the soft white bread of a sausage sandwich.

The second-hand bookshop

A second-hand bookshop draws me in as a moth to a candle. Each shop is a small shrine to the power and beauty of words. Tightly packed shelves of old hardback novels; heavy tomes on art and design; teetering piles of poetry. There are copies of the *Children's Encylopedia* used as a doorstop and wooden crates of paperbacks going for a song. Some are rare, with a price to match, others a fraction of their original cost. A book for everyone, I guess.

Yes, it's the thought of words put together with such care, the pages whose surface has been worn by years of handling; the tired bindings and torn-edged covers where a book has been in less kind hands than it should. (A chance to give a damaged book a kinder home.) But even more, it is the smell that makes me want to enter every second-hand bookshop I pass. A smell that is dusty, a cross between an old leather saddle and a country church.

Holding a book that has been read by others feels like I am about to make a new friend, a story that someone else has enjoyed and is now passing on to me. I sniff the pages (a lifelong habit that borders on perversion), admire their foxing, the pages freckled with rust, their fading spines. I restore the occasional puppy-eared corner, bent over by a vandal, worried how uncomfortable it might be for the book.

Sometimes the book carries a tale even before you turn the first page. A gift, a love story, complete with signatures and dates: 'Happy Birthday' or 'Saw this and thought of you'; 'To my dearest Helena'. Some books open with a letterpress bookplate, 'From the Library of ...' Occasionally the title page comes with the author's signature or an inscription, 'To Betty with love.' I have a few that were once part of a library, one of which is complete with its lending card.

Annotations tell a story too. My aunt put a simple pencil tick in every Mills & Boon romance she borrowed from the public library so she could spot those she had read. An entire literary lifetime of stories of 'doctor falls in love with nurse'. I have a cookery book, picked up in a charming shop near Kew Gardens, that is annotated by the previous owner. A recipe for 'Moist Fruit Cake' comes with the grumpy addition, 'No it isn't.'

I sometimes want to buy a book simply because no one else has taken it home, like a lost kitten. But surely a book is amongst friends in a second-hand bookshop; perhaps I should leave it there? I should add that I am more donor than buyer. I take unwanted review copies to charity bookshops in the hope that they will find a friend and make money for a good cause whilst they are at it.

Ginger cake is perhaps the most magical cake of all. I bless the way you don't have to cream the sugar and butter together and gently beat in the eggs or sieve in the flour. I like the fact that you just put the syrup and black treacle, sugar and butter in a pan and melt them. That you then stir in the eggs, flour and spice, pour the runny batter into a cake tin and bake it. Literally magic.

The singing pots

In Wales, at the opening of Steve Harrison's kiln. (Correctly, the term is to 'crack' the kiln.) The bricks are removed and the vessels within reveal themselves. They are lifted out, one by one, still warm, like loaves. These are shallow, salt-glaze pots, made to serve food, in hues of softest blue and brown, some the colour of clotted cream.

Steve hands each of them to me, hot from the kiln, and I place them tenderly on the walls and piles of broken bricks around us. I am silent, in awe of each piece. As they cool, the pots start to sing. A soft, tinkling sound like wind chimes in a breeze or ice cracking on a pond. A hundred pots, ping, ping, tinkle, tinkle.

One of the beakers is a little different from its kiln mates, the same round shape and soft colours but the glaze is more crackled and a more luminous blue, and as such it stands apart. The 'orange-peel' feel of the salt-glaze exterior feels more pronounced to the touch, like rubbing your fingers over braille. I say nothing, but I can't take my eyes off it.

We eat roast pumpkin with miso for dinner that Julia, Steve's wife, has cooked, then go for a walk in the dark.

After breakfast the following day we pack, and Steve hands me a parcel. It is the blue pot to take home.

A broken and much-loved teapot, its inside stained brown with tannin, the pieces arranged on an oval celadon dish. An artwork born out of a disaster.

Ink on my fingers

At school we filled our pens from a bottle of blue-black ink. I do to this day. And though the pen is now a Pelikan and the ink is Iroshizuku, the details are very much the same.

I kept my school pen, a simple black Osmiroid, long after most gave theirs up for biros and rollerballs. Until well into my thirties that pen and its much-worn italic nib slept in my pencil case, woken daily to scribble a note in my kitchen diary or to annotate a recipe. Then, one day, it wasn't. Losing a pen you have had for most of your life is a bereavement of sorts.

A fountain pen, rather than a rollerball, pencil or biro, remains my favoured instrument with which to keep a note or structure a shopping list; to address an envelope or write a thank-you letter. Yes, it is the soft scratching of nib on paper, the scent of the ink, the shape of my handwriting on the page, but there is something else. Whilst filling its polished black barrel and wiping the pen's neck and nib, I rather like getting ink on my fingers.

Smudges of school blue-black Quink and the Tsuki-yo (translation: 'moonlight') I now use are as permanent a part of my hands as any tattoo. Even scrubbed, there is always a faint trail of blue-black on my fingertips, like veins on a Stilton. That said, I have the finger-prints of a ghost. Index, middle, ring and little finger, even my thumb, have almost invisible papillary ridges. The arches, loops, ridges and whorls are as smooth as vellum. Indeed, I often wonder if I should have made a career as a burglar or even a serial killer. (Oh, and never stand behind me in the queue at immigration; it takes twenty attempts to get the machine to recognise my faint imprint.)

The road map of blue-black at the end of my thumb and index finger is strangely reassuring. It would probably always be there if I didn't spend so much time washing up. But then that, too, is a pleasure. Ink stains, and the tiny suede 'nib-wipe' I carry in my pencil case, probably make me look old-fashioned, yet videos of calligraphy on YouTube are much watched, as are comparisons of different nibs and inks. It is one of the more relaxing internet rabbit holes down which to explore. Watching a calligrapher's exquisite swirls and swooshes of ink on paper is mesmerising.

I prefer a dry ink, the slightly viscous liquid that flows slowly from the nib. Fill my pen with a wet, juicy ink and my words will feather on the page, like lipstick on cracked lips. The same effect you see when writing on cheap, often recycled paper, with tiny threads of ink appearing round the letters. Wet ink will bleed through the paper too, or ghost, leaving apparitions of letters visible on the other side.

An old, straight-backed Chinese scholar's chair, to the right of my desk, and on it a pile of card folders the colour of toffee. Holding the 'manuscript of the moment', they have, over the years, taken on an almost velvet feel, their edges worn from years of use.

A magical dance

It is my second-earliest memory. Men dancing, some with antlers on their heads, others with ribbons and tiny, rattling bells. There were hats garlanded with wildflowers and the steady, haunting beat of a drum. The rhythmic clack-clack-clack of wood on wood. I have long assumed it was the Abbots Bromley Horn Dance, as the village was just an hour's drive away from my childhood home.

This is where things get misty. I have a crystal-clear picture of some of the players wearing masks and long coats decorated with ribbons, which doesn't quite fit in with the traditional Horn Dance but seems more like that of the Mummers, which would also account for the knocking wood. I recollect the fields around being crisp and toasted, so it was late summer, and regard the event as being curiously unsettling.

I left feeling as if I had witnessed something magical yet – to a young and fragile mind – strangely sinister. This memory, dream-like now, is from when I was six or seven. I am happy that it haunts me to this day.

One of the many good things about getting older is that I can push a plate away when I have had enough without any feeling of guilt. I am a big boy now and don't need to finish everything before I can get down.

Getting better

I was rather looking forward to the general anaesthetic. I have been lulled to sleep for bits and pieces of surgery four or five times now and loved every minute of it. The anaesthesia, that is; I knew nothing of the surgery. I awaited the hushed, there-there words of the anaesthetist that fell softly on the air, the sensation of the pre-med, as if my body was filling with tiny warm bubbles, the notion of falling, falling, falling into deep, marshmallow-soft pillows. I drifted, slightly queasy, in and out of consciousness. A paper bag on a wave.

It goes without saying I was also looking forward to coming out from the anaesthetic. The oh-so-delicious feeling that I am still alive, that I need not have rewritten my will in a last-minute panic – that, to put it bluntly, I am back. Soft, misty light comes through the tight white window blinds, a puddle of water glistens on the floor, which I hope is from the open window, not me, and the room is illuminated now, in minimalist black and white, like a Hiroshi Sugimoto photograph. I wiggle my toes, then my legs, and then run my fingers gently over my soft dressings. Everything appears to be working. A slow, warm feeling of euphoria tingles through my body followed by the rare feeling that for once nothing matters, that everything on my to-do list is suddenly of no consequence and that anyone needing anything from me is just going to have to wait.

Hospital, with its crisp white sheets and smiling nurses, feels like a holiday of sorts. Yes, the pain gets the better of the drugs sometimes, there is the frustration of being told what to do and when to eat, but there is also the quietly blissful feeling of (whisper it) being looked after, of being safe in other people's hands. Or, to put it another way, of being someone else's problem rather than your own. As a guy who rises before six every day, I rather enjoy being told to stay put, trapped by intravenous drips and a high-sided hospital bed. Yes, there are dressings to be changed and blood pressures to be taken, medications to swallow and the peering and gentle prodding of experts. All of which I find strangely comforting.

The days go by and there are moments of angst and, yes, pain. But you tick off the little challenges, the one-step-at-a-time list; the small accomplishments to which you rise each day. You soak up the sympathy as a sponge pudding soaks up custard but you carry on as best you can, even push yourself.

And then one day it slowly hits you, in much the same way as the warm bubbles of the anaesthetist's pre-med filled your veins: YOU ARE GETTING BETTER. There is a warm rush of energy, a rejuvenation, you are suddenly fizzing with positivity and clarity. For the first time in ages, anything, absolutely anything, seems possible. And you know what? It probably is.

There are no rules with Christmas pudding. You need not wait until you have had your main course. You can even – and I thoroughly recommend this – eat it cold, for breakfast.

Finding perfume

Smell everything: the single, open-petalled rose in the early-morning light, the Marsala-tinted notes of Christmas dinner and the coffee beans being ground for our first cup of the day. These are things we do without thinking, a sensory knee jerk. We know what to expect. But who can leave it there? In many ways our sense of smell is underused, and yet there is so much pleasure to be had, so many doors to open, labyrinths to explore.

I sniff the pages of every book, the fur on the cat's head, each jumper, scarf and woolly hat, the spices in my grinder, the tea in my caddies. It is an impulse, a lifelong habit. I may not always listen or see things, especially when I have no wish to, but I will always use my sense of smell, taking in the olfactory notes of every room, each and every object and person. Yes, I will smell you.

Some of us remember the colour of people's eyes, the tint of their hair, their shoes. I remember their smell. Hands and smell are what I notice at first meeting. Hands that are gnarled and scarred, or smooth and pale like those of a porcelain doll. Hands that are chubby and those that are not. There are hands I will not shake and some I wished I hadn't. Yet my instinct is always to breathe in when I meet someone. It is how I first take their measure. A fresh citrus cologne, the warm and comforting hint of potting shed or of fresh sweat on clean flesh. You will be remembered for the odour you carry long after I have forgotten what shoes you were wearing.

As I said, I smell everything. The cinnamon in the jar, the fruity scent of dark chocolate, the leather interior of a classic car. I once climbed aboard an old school bus for a television documentary

348

whose 1960s carpet-covered seats brought back the happiness and angst of my childhood in one huge, dusty cloud.

It is rare to come across a new smell. An essence you have never experienced before. It is like opening the lid to a treasure chest. The first time I smelled the soft, powdery rocks of Somalian frankincense James brought back from travelling; the whiff of a broken dahlia stem or inhaled green osmanthus-flower tea was like stepping through the back of the wardrobe into Narnia. Likewise crocuses, charcoal and umeshu, the citrine-hued Japanese plum wine.

There are smells we never forget, the fragrances that imprint themselves on us as permanently as a tattoo on our skin. That first smoky, dusty smell of an antique shop; the ink in the bottle as I filled my school fountain pen; of coriander leaf in a fish soup in a bistro in Paris; begonias in my father's greenhouse and early-morning snow in the Dolomites. Something you smelled as a child – of phlox on a summer's evening, a ripe melon at a picnic or the energising sap from a Christmas tree – can be carried around like a talisman.

My parents wore the same perfume and aftershave all their lives. I was headed down the same road: for most of my life I had worn an Italian cologne with a singular citrus presence. Its light, clean, almost biting freshness appealed, as did its story and androgynous character. It had never actually occurred to me that, while it had slowly become part of my presence throughout my twenties and thirties, it might not actually suit me. Bergamot- and citrus-based fragrances generally work better on a darker skin than mine.

I am a firm believer that someone should not be able to smell your perfume until they are close enough to touch you. Almost all the big-name fragrances can fill a room with just one squirt. (My golden rule of never wearing anything you can buy at duty free isn't as snobby as it sounds. Who wants to smell like everyone else?) Whereas I am happy to change my perfume to suit the occasion, the season, my state of mind, having a scent you wear almost as a uniform is strangely comforting and makes the excursions into others even more of an adventure.

The top notes of most fragrances are delightfully fleeting, which is also the problem with buying something on first meeting. Finding a new perfume is probably like finding a new friend: you need to take your time to see what is left behind once the top and middle notes have vanished. Like polite conversation, you have to know what lies beneath the initial shallowness of a first meeting. In fact, you might wonder about the purpose of the top notes at all, so quickly do they disappear.

I have never been drawn to the more masculine scents, the tobacco and leather colognes targeted at the male shopper that are the olfactory answer to beating your chest like a drum. (Looking at you, Calvin and Tom.) Subtle they are not. Like a paint that doesn't change with the light, they smell the same all day. I wanted a perfume that slowly unfolded rather than stayed the same as when it came from the bottle.

It is fascinating to compare the ingredients in your favourite perfumes. When stripped down into top, heart and base notes, I was surprised how many of mine contained the same ingredients. Vetiver, juniper, frankincense and oakmoss were often there. I am apparently also drawn to Egyptian geranium. Vetiver is found in Haiti and India, made from the root of a species of grass and known for its ability to induce calm and tranquillity. It is described by Neil Chapman, author of *Perfume*, as 'emotionally cooling'. It seems my favourites are those that induce a sense of serenity and calm, which comes as little surprise.

Taking a walk

I have the sense of direction of a lettuce. I have lost count of how many times, even in the friendly company of a map, I have walked for hours in completely the wrong direction. It is one of the things I am most embarrassed about, this geographical muddle I get into from time to time. That, and my ability to fall, slip or trip at will.

I regularly walked back from school. A journey that took me across fields, over cowpats and puddles and through woods. Sixty years on, I walk to the shops, and even back from dinner in town. When I'm away I walk all day, and often late into the night. Whether I dawdle or march, I tend to get to wherever I am going on foot. It is my wish and hope that this will never change.

On the occasions when I couldn't walk – when I fell on holiday in Nice and had to be wheeled to the plane in a wheelchair or when, more recently, I came home from minor surgery and had to negotiate the stairs to bed step by slow step, each movement taking what felt like a lifetime – I appreciated each footfall more than ever.

Walking grounds me, literally and spiritually. If I am stuck with a tricky paragraph, I will step softly around the garden to unravel the knot of words in my head. Should I need to think through a dilemma or even make the most straightforward of decisions, I tend to do so on foot. That said, the best walks are not those in my garden or even in my local streets, 'my manor'. The best walks are those on unfamiliar territory where at some point I am briefly lost, only to find a recognisable house or tree and know I am once again in safe hands. Even better, perhaps, is to take a favourite path and feel the warm fuzz of familiarity, finding it barely changed since last time.

Over the years, my walking eyeline has had to change. A lifetime of looking up at parapets and chimneys has been lost with the need to watch my every step, to spot each curb and loose paving stone long before I go sprawling. Not everything about growing older is a joy. Just most of it. I can still hear my father's words, 'You had better watch your step, lad' – but they carry a different meaning now.

Most of my walking is done away from home, when I will happily walk thirty thousand steps around Antwerp or Edinburgh, Bath or Budapest. Morning walks that become afternoon walks, my steps slowing with the ticking of the clock. My pace finally spurred on with the knowledge that in another thousand paces I can collapse into a chair in the hotel bar.

Threads

I have a deep affection for some of my clothes. Mostly jumpers, coats and boots – they are so easy to love, but pretty much everything is treated with the sort of care that may surprise those who made them, sitting at the work benches, cutting, stitching and knitting. I look after them, even cherish them.

There is an extraordinary sadness about discarding an ageing jumper or a threadbare coat, a cardigan that has unravelled over the years, ravaged by moths or stained whilst making dinner (beetroot again, turmeric, pomegranate!). And I do feel there is a bond, even an unspoken intimacy with our clothes – after all, they touch us, they live next to our skin – though I doubt they care much about it.

In turn, I expect much from my clothes, and their life is measured in years rather than months. In the case of a waxed anorak or a donkey jacket, my clothes have been known to last decades – so long in fact that I often can't even remember when I first acquired them. I quietly curse those massive companies that sell clothes designed for a short life. Disposable, unsustainable fashion.

Much thought is given to my clothes' demise. Rarely is anything thrown out of my wardrobe until it is long past being useful as a duster. (Old, soft, cotton T-shirts make great dusters.) Tell me, please, I am not the only one who has put something aside to throw away only to dig it out later and start wearing it again? Clothing is more than just wool or cotton, linen or leather. It is about comfort and survival, clothes give us confidence and help us heal, they allow us to deal with life and all it throws at us. They keep us company through thick and thin, like a good friend.

I have a vast jumper, long and shapeless, that comes out when I am especially tired or under the weather. A pair of jeans so holey I would probably be arrested if I wore them outside the house, yet so soft and comfortable I cannot bear to part with them. Yet they are only clothes. So why does putting an old jumper in the recycling bin feels like an abandonment, a betrayal? Why does losing a scarf or a single glove (usually the right one) feel as if I have hurt it?

'Bye ... something new is taking your place.' I wouldn't even want old and new to meet, to nudge one another on the shelf. I cannot remember getting rid of anything simply because I grew tired of it.

Repairs are more than examples of frugality, they are a way of letting your clothes know how much you respect them. A repair is beautiful, like a scar. Its presence enhances rather than diminishes. A line of darning will never stop me loving a jumper; in fact, I will probably love it all the more. I particularly cherish repairs when they are proud rather than hidden, when a complementary colour of thread or wool is used rather than a near match. The fact that repaired works are shown in exhibitions like works of art makes me happy beyond words.

The bliss of a muted palette

If everyone's life has a palette, mine is muted: grey, brown, green, deep inky blue. I cook in a kitchen with soft, lime-washed walls, and one of my most-worn pieces of clothing is a voluminous cardigan the colour of clotted cream. A home, a wardrobe and a garden in every shade of smoke, moss, parchment and ink. And yet what I eat is exactly the opposite. Vivid greens and bright crimsons fill my fridge; the larder has jars and bottles with every shade of pink and violet, orange and magenta. The more colourful and vibrant the food I eat, the happier I am. I have just made a salad of milky-white burrata, purple basil and peaches the colours of a sunset. Breakfast involved melon, wine-red raspberries and nuggets of crimson pomegranate. Eat the rainbow, they say, and I do.

Surrounded by gentle tones and hushed voices, I am happy, and yet also find myself mesmerised by colour – the carnival echo of a jug of dahlias, a scarlet vending machine full of jelly beans or the neon pinks and greens of Shinjuku, the world's busiest pedestrian crossing, where as many as three thousand people can cross the road at any one time. (I have been caught in the middle of this on more than one occasion, yet there was no panic attack, no frantic hurry to find a deserted backstreet. I just accepted my fate to be briefly swept along like flotsam on a flooding river.)

For every calming brown and grey or dark green, a flash of crimson, pink or orange is welcome too. I garden this way, a magenta rose or a tangerine geum planted against the deep green of a yew hedge or a cheeky orange trumpet on a pale narcissus twinkling like a bird's beak from the undergrowth. A flash of vivid colour, be it in the garden, on the wall or on the plate, will annoy or energise, depending on the mood; or perhaps its presence simply allows me to appreciate the sleepy, hushed, muted palette of my life all the more.

Moon bathing

The moon is full again tonight, a shimmering silver and ice-blue globe, bathing the tips of the trees in ghostly white light. I am in the hills near Kurama, but it is a light I have seen in the Hebrides, Lapland and on the Cornish coast.

London, where I live now, is not the best place to witness the moon and its magic. Too many other luminous intrusions. 'Moons I have known' might be a good title for an autobiography and I would certainly label a few as unforgettable, though that is possibly because of a state of mind rather than the state of the moon. More intrepid travellers than myself will have memories of their most spectacular waxing and waning moons, full, crescent or sickle, but mine exist mostly in my imagination. In particular the image that has been carried since childhood, of the moon that lit my path through a dense forest of fir trees guiding me to a log cabin, where I arrived to find the table laid just for me.

The appearance of the full moon comes with a cast that includes ghosts and werewolves, vampires and fairies, lunatics and late-night revellers, but also this extraordinary light. An incandescence that picks out the white petals of certain garden flowers – nicotiana, the spikes of actaea and echinops, allium snow globes and the dancing white fairies that are aquilegia. The best of these is probably the appropriately named sea holly, Miss Willmott's Ghost, with its ruff of grey spikes that appear to glow silver in moonlight. The name was given not for this delightful feature, but for the late gardener's habit of secretly distributing its seeds wherever she went. I know of a writer who does the same with wild poppies.

There is something nurturing about eating green leaves that have been planted according to the position of the moon. The understanding that the grower has recognised that lunar and planetary changes can affect the quality of what we eat. Vegetables, and in particular leafy greens, that are planted according to the rhythm of the Earth's movements. The notion of vegetables seasoned with as much magic as salt and pepper appeals to me.

Unlike the brash, punch-you-in-the-eye sun, the moon holds secrets. The most difficult photograph in my collection is a night seascape. At first sight, there is nothing to witness but jet-black. Lit by an expert, gently rippling waves slowly appear across the lower half of the picture. Then, gradually, a horizon, together with a sliver of the moon on the black water. Badly lit, as it is in my house, you can see almost nothing. I can't help but feel that this was always the photographer's intention, a picture that reveals itself only to a few.

Tonight's moon is a good moon. Nothing bad could happen under its sleepy, benevolent gaze. No elves and goblins are abroad tonight.